HOW TO SURVIVE IN THE IB DIPLOMA PROGRAM

HOW TO SURVIVE IN THE IB DIPLOMA PROGRAM

THE DEFINITIVE GUIDE TO SUCCESS IN
THE INTERNATIONAL BACCALAUREATE [IB]

**INESSA KULBARISOVA
ANNIQUE QUARLES VAN UFFORD
ALEXANDER ZOUEV**

Copyright © 2024 Zouev Publishing. All rights reserved.

No part of this book may be used or reproduced in any manner whatsoever without written permission, except in the case of brief quotations embodied in critical articles or reviews.

Published 2024

ISBN 978-1-7385371-1-2, paperback.

This book is dedicated to you, the IB student.

Thank you to the dozens of IB teachers, IB coordinators, and IB alumni who edited and proofread this guide. We are extremely grateful for your feedback and advice while writing this book.

TABLE OF CONTENTS

YES, YOU CAN	1
WHY DO 1 IN 5 STUDENTS FAIL?	13
HOW TO DO THE BASICS	25
HOW TO CHOOSE YOUR SUBJECTS	41
HOW TO SUCCEED IN THE IB CLASSROOM	69
HOW TO WIN FRIENDS AND INFLUENCE TEACHERS	87
HOW TO USE THE INTERNET	103
HOW (NOT) TO USE CHAT GPT	117
HOW TO HACK YOUR GDC AND FORMULA BOOK	123
HOW TO ACHIEVE FULL MARKS ON YOUR IA	131
HOW TO USE PAST PAPERS	149
HOW TO REVISE LIKE A PRO	163
HOW TO TAKE EXAMS LIKE A BOSS	185
HOW TO COMPLETE CAS	201
HOW TO GET ALL 3 BONUS POINTS	213
HOW TO CHEAT	221
HOW TO OPTIMIZE IBY1	229
HOW TO FIND THE PERFECT IB TUTOR	237
HOW TO REST AND RECOVER	243
HOW TO SURVIVE POST-IB	249
WTF IS AN IBDP? YOUR GUIDE TO IB ACRONYMS	267

CHAPTER 1

YES, YOU CAN

"I used to have a life. Then I started cheating on it with the IB, and then me and life got a divorce."

Congratulations on picking up the only book you will ever need to pass the IB Diploma program!

Not only will you pass, but you will succeed to your full potential, and certainly have a very good chance of obtaining the coveted 40+ IB points total.

Whether you are a student in need of guidance, a teacher looking to find new teaching techniques, or simply an interested reader – you will find that this short, but to-the-point book meets all of your expectations.

By opening these pages, you are already one step closer to logging onto that IB results website after your exams and seeing a nice big juicy: 'DIPLOMA OBTAINED'.

INTRODUCTION

Allow me to start off with a personal anecdote.

Let's rewind back to 2005 – I was 15 years old, and I was just finishing pre-IB at the Antwerp International School in Belgium. My report card for the 2nd term of school that year had the following grades:

Science: C

Math: B-

English: C

Foreign Lang: C-

Geography: D

Art: A

As you can imagine, I was not the brightest kid, nor did I show much initiative or 'apply myself'. I was not looking forward to entering what was considered the most rigorous high school diploma program in the world...

Fast forward to two and a half years later, and these were my final results in the IB Diploma:

HL Mathematics: **7**

HL Economics: **7**

HL Physics: **6**

HL Geography: **7**

SL Dutch: **6**

SL English Lang. and Lit: **7**

TOK: **A**

EE: **A**

Bonus points: **3/3**

Total Points: **43/45**

DIPLOMA OBTAINED.

So, how exactly did this transformation happen?

How did I go from a very average sophomore student in high school, to scoring amongst the top 1% of IB students for the 2007 year?

There was certainly a steep learning curve, and I had to teach myself how to play what I like to call the 'IB game'.

What exactly is this IB game, I hear you ask? Well, like all high school programmes, there are certain specifics that you can use to exploit and 'hack' the assessments in order to maximize your grade.

This book will shed light on some of those secret tips and tricks I used to make my transformation complete.

This book is not a substitute for studying in school – it's about making the best use of the knowledge provided here so that you can impress examiners at crucial moments. It's about picking up a dozen extra vital marks here and there in enough assessments to lift you into the next grade boundary.

It's certainly not magic, although it might feel like it. And while I can tell you what things you can do, I can't make you the kind of person to do them.

However, learning the rules of the very complex game of the IB Diploma can make you a better player. Like any game, there will be different views about how to get the best results, so it's going to be sensible to listen to all of the different advice and decide for yourself.

Most importantly, this is NOT the official IBO guide to anything, although everything here certainly fits within IBO policies and rules.

WHO IS THIS BOOK FOR?

Let's make one thing clear: this is not a textbook. You will not find any syllabus specific educational material here. I have tried to make this guidebook accessible to everyone, whether you are totally new to the world of the IB, or an IB Year 2 student a few months away from your final exams.

This book is packed full of information about the crucial aspects of the International Baccalaureate Diploma Programme, and it is written by an IB expert with 12 years of experience, along with two recent alumni from the '45 club'. It is a treasure trove for anybody who needs to know anything IB related.

The style and tone of this book make it more accessible to a student in the program, as opposed to an IB parent (please excuse my language throughout) or an IB teacher, or even an IB coordinator (although I would not be very surprised if there are any of those reading these pages...)

This book is for *you,* and your classmates. By all means, let them borrow these pages, and the same goes for your parents. I honestly feel like the advice in this book can be understood relatively well by almost anyone who is familiar with the programme.

HOW DO I USE THIS BOOK?

It is my hope that this book will not be something you breeze through once and relegate to the darkest and dustiest corner of your bookshelf. Rather, I sincerely hope this book has insights that will be relevant to all stages of your IB journey and that you can periodically come back to it and visit the relevant chapters of whatever it is you are struggling with. From selecting your IB subjects, to wrestling with the EE, to bullsh*ting your TOK presentation. It is my hope that you keep this book by your bedside like a mini IB bible.

Use it from time to time when you're starting on presentations, or Internal Assessment, or exam revision or whatever is important and IB-related. If you read it all at once, you'll forget most of it, especially if your memory is extra shitty like mine.

WHY THIS BOOK AND NOT OTHERS?

In recent years the market for IB 'help' material has become greatly saturated with both recommendable and some avoidable books being published.

Thus, before going into the details of how to maximize your IB points total, let me put your mind at ease by providing a little background.

Having completed my IB diploma in 2007 with an overall score of 43, I went on to read Economics and Management at the University of Oxford.

At this point, some of you may begin to ask whether it would make more sense to obtain advice from someone who has gotten a 45 on their IB, or better yet a qualified IB teacher who has decades of experience teaching the program. The answer to that question is: maybe! Which is why for this new edition of the book, I have enlisted the help of not one, but two wonderful contributors who both scored the maximum 45 marks in the 2023 exam session.

WHY SHOULD WE LISTEN TO YOU?

I know exactly how it feels to be an average student struggling with the program and looking for all the right resources and answers with minimal effort. The student that gets 45 will most of the time be someone who has great natural intelligence, but probably devoted most of his/her teenage years to studying revision guides 24/7 rather than living a normal teen life.

In other words, it's not me or you. What I can offer you is fool-proof advice and techniques on how to obtain 7's in most of your subjects without having to work relentlessly and waste countless hours staying up and memorizing useless information.

In truth, I am the type of person that does not like to miss a party. I can recall that five weeks before the start of exams some of my friends and I went out on Friday, Saturday and Sunday only to have to sit mocks the following week. Having a mind-blowing hangover on the morning of Senior Day three weeks before exams is another fond memory.

The point here is that you need not drop all your social gatherings, athletic events and personal hobbies in order to survive in the world of IB. In fact, you don't need to drop any.

Some of the most successful IB candidates I know were all captains of a sports team, busy jumping from one relationship to another, or recovering every other Saturday morning from excessive drinking.

Their secret? Natural intelligence? Perhaps. But in most of the cases it was simply an ability to be efficient, hard-working when necessary, and only doing what was essential in order to get the grade they need. No more, no less. All of these tips you can expect to find in this book.

If you follow the advice put forth in this book correctly and put in some effort and determination, I firmly believe that you can obtain a total of 40 or above – irrespective of any 'natural' intelligence.

If, however, you are someone less ambitious, looking to score 7's in some of your subjects whilst maintaining a pass in others, then you will simply need to flip to the chapters that suit your needs.

WHAT IS MY STORY?

As aforementioned, the two points I missed out on to get a 45 where due to a 6 in Physics (Higher Level) and a 6 in English (Standard Level). Looking back, I do blame myself for not following my own advice enough to get that 7 in Physics (or better yet, choosing f*cking Biology instead like a normal person), however the English I have no regrets about. I tried my best and did what I could but did not get a 7 (a large part of me blames my useless English teacher at the time who provided literally zero support).

Unfortunately, this book will not teach you how to get a perfect score of 45/45 and place you in the top 0.01% of candidates. For that, I recommend our other more detailed (400+ page) book – *45 Tips, Tricks, and Secrets for the Successful IB student.*

I know plenty of people who have obtained this amazing feat. However, almost all admit to having had a slice of good fortune somewhere along their path to perfection. With most university offers capped at around 40 points there is also no need to get a perfect score - unless you are the ultimate perfectionist.

CAN I BE AN IB SUCCESS?

No matter how little natural academic ability you have, I firmly believe that with minimal effort on your part, you simply cannot fail if you have read and used this book. There is no effortless way to achieve the grades that you want. There are, however, ways that will save you time, effort and money, yet still let you reach your maximum potential and get the grades of your dreams.

For those of you reading to find any tips on plagiarism, cheating or any other non-ethical method to get a higher grade – you will have to look elsewhere. My tips and techniques are 100% in line with the rules and regulations of the IB guidelines. Understandably, there will be critics amongst parents and teachers who suggest that a lot of what I endorse is in some ways non-ethical and not in accordance with what the IB preaches. These arguments lack merit. I would argue that nothing I advocate in this book even borders on the moral grey area.

Countless students are getting the top grades and succeeding without succumbing to becoming lifeless bookworms. One needs to understand and appreciate that there is "cheating" and then there are "tactical and efficient study techniques", and there is a thick line separating the two concepts.

This book will ultimately teach you to become masters of manipulating the resources at your disposal efficiently and tactically, without having to resort to anything that can be regarded as 'cheating'.

CHANGE YOUR MINDSET

What is essential before we begin is that you throw away all preconceived notions about the IB as being something scary, elitist, incredibly demanding and impossible to crack.

I was once amongst you, but after finding out that the IB is just as easy to decipher as the A-levels, the AP programs, or the SATs – I became fearless.

This is an essential stepping-stone in your long road to IB success.

Yes, your non-IB friends will call you an overachieving geek. Yes, you may find you have more assignments and tests than the other "normal" kids. And yes, there will be times when you wonder why your parents/teachers would ever want to put you through so much traumatizing pain. However, one should not fear. The techniques in this book will ensure that your two-year ride will be amongst the most memorable and fun two years of your life. It certainly was for me.

Some of you may ask why I didn't produce a book outlining the techniques and methods of success in subjects I myself actually studied (HL: Economics, Mathematics, Geography, SL: English, Dutch, Physics) rather than making an entire manual outlining all the various subjects in less detail. The truth is that most of the techniques I use overlap from subject to subject.

Hence, I am able to offer a greater variety of advice to students not necessarily taking those subjects, but still struggling with similar problems. This way the book can offer advice on issues that other more specialized IB books cannot. Namely: study advice, internal assessment advice, past paper advice, and general IB work advice.

The second reason I tried to avoid being too detailed about the specifics of the course is simply because there is already an abundance of good information out there.

Although I could spend chapters discussing the detailed syllabus of the IB Economics course, it would be a wasted effort as there are a handful of brilliantly written textbooks on the matter already.

What is missing, however, is general advice that applies across subjects and helps you become an efficient and well-rounded IB student. This book aims to fill that void.

LOOK OUT FOR THE PRO TIPS

Scattered throughout this book you will occasionally find the following:

> **Pro Tip:** this is an example of a Pro Tip – make sure to make notes in the margin of this book. Also, highlight all the important stuff that you will most likely forget.

Basically, these are tips that I couldn't fit into any paragraph.

Most of the time they are little-known secrets or words of wisdom.

Other times, they are pretty obvious.

Your job is to not only read them but imprint them into your memory so that you use them throughout your IB journey.

A LITTLE REALITY CHECK

I wanted to start this book off on a very important note. The IB is hard, and very time-consuming. However, this does not mean that you are going to have to invest every minute of your day on IB tasks. On the contrary, I am a firm believer in the importance of living a balanced lifestyle.

Personally, I saw students that submerged themselves in coursework, and gave up any and all hobbies or social life. Although some of them did end up doing well, I still wonder if all their sacrifices were worth it. I, on the other hand, focused on balancing my time. I made sure not to neglect my schoolwork, always staying up to date with my assignments and notes.

However, I was still part of multiple sports teams, and took time to hang out with friends and go out. It was this balance that allowed me to score well, as all other activities were a way for me to de-stress and make lasting memories. I won't go into all the scientific evidence behind exercise and socializing as a motivator for good work but trust me when I say that no IB grade is worth sacrificing the best two years of high school.

CHAPTER 2

WHY DO 1 IN 5 STUDENTS FAIL?

"You shall not pass" – Gandalf, on the IB

I know. It's scary, and it's daunting.

However, that statistic is unfortunately not an exaggeration.

Let's have a look at the relevant excerpt from the IBO Statistical Bulletin for the May 2023 Examinations:

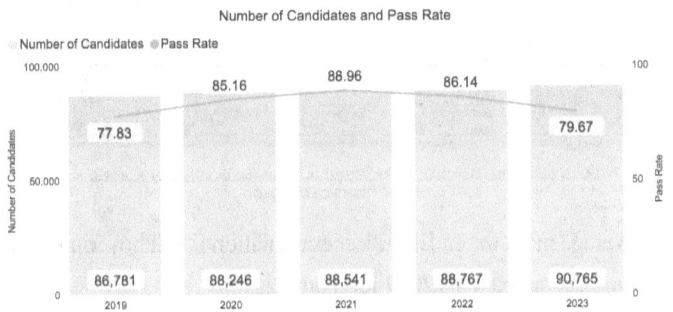

source: https://www.ibo.org/globalassets/new-structure/about-the-ib/pdfs/dp-cp-provisional-statistical-bulletin-may-2023.pdf

We can note several things:

1. The number of candidates is still steadily increasing.
2. The **pass rate was 79.67** in 2023, and thereby significantly lower than the previous years.
3. The IB has returned to its original "difficulty level" after a 3-year period with abnormally high passing rates due to COVID-19

This means that out of the 90,765 candidates that took the diploma in 2023, **20.33% failed,** which is **18,452 students** that had to load up their results page and see that they did obtain the diploma that they had been working so hard for.

Furthermore, with regards to the average score:

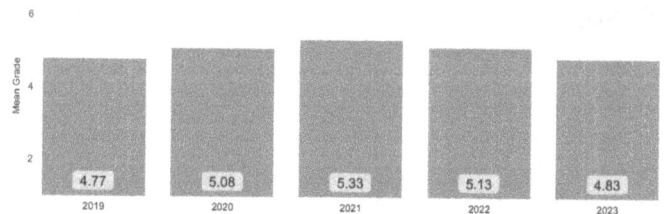

source: https://www.ibo.org/globalassets/new-structure/about-the-ib/pdfs/dp-cp-provisional-statistical-bulletin-may-2023.pdf

The average mark for an IB subject examination is still hovering below a 5, having decreased to its 2019-level once again.

The trend is clear: during COVID-19, IB students performed much better than before. M23 was the first session to return the IB back to its usual challenging level.

The grade inflation seen can be attributed to the modifications made for them, such as not sitting the exams in 2020, no paper 2's for language A classes, no paper 3's for most science courses, etc.

Although some may argue that this is unfair, we have to think back to the circumstances in which some of these candidates took the exam. However, it can be questioned if the modifications were perhaps too severe: the average score increased by almost one whole point globally!

The average total score for students has actually risen slightly from 2019, however it is still roughly 30 points.

We, nonetheless, are going to be aiming for much better than that!

The key takeaway here is that the IB has high failing rates, and that there are no more COVID modifications that might make your exam session easier.

So why do so many people still fail the IB?

To try and answer that is the aim of this book, with each chapter addressing a component that I believe is critical to achieving success in the diploma.

There are however a few more factors that need to be considered in order to understand why there is such a high failure rate.

THE AMERICA SITUATION

Having done a little research, it does seem that the '1 in 5' statistic is more of a trend in the US than it is in other parts of the world. There are several reasons for this.

A lot of US schools just try their best to get their kids into college, and once the unconditional offer rolls in – that student switches off.

There are a lot of circumstances where the kids take the diploma for whatever reason but only care about how taking the classes look on their transcripts. For example, my friend transferred from an international school where there were prestigious national universities that only cared about IB candidacy and strong English skills, to a US school where most kids go to US colleges.

In both cases, once college admissions were in, the effort from kids vanished. Most US schools (except maybe the very prestigious) don't seem to care too much about IB results. By the time IB exams roll around most Americans are already accepted to college so there is very little motivation to try hard in exams. This is what (primarily) leads to the abnormally high failure rate.

THE IB IS NOT FOR EVERYONE

Before you even embark on your IB adventure, you need to decide if the IB is for you. By that I mean, is the IB diploma the bridge you need to get to the next point in your life – whatever that may be?

Depending on where you are located geographically, what your future career ambitions are, and what school choices are on offer, you may be faced with the task of deciding whether the IB is worth it in your individual situation.

> **Pro Tip:** make the decision early on if you wish to do the full IB Diploma. There is no shame in choosing a better-suited high school curriculum to follow. The sooner you make this decision, the better.

There is a good reason that the IB program has such a notoriously difficult and rigorous reputation around the world. The upside is that you are encouraged to think independently and learn how to think. You also become more culturally aware as you develop a second (or in some cases, third) language, and you will be able to engage with people in an increasingly globalized and rapidly changing world.

I know it seems crazy to be thinking about all of this when you are 15 years old and don't even know much about university and what you wish to study, but the IB is a huge decision and one you should not take lightly. Our main advice here is to do your research. I can only give general help, each case will vary on the specifics, so pick up that phone and start calling potential universities to find out their recognition status of the IB Diploma.

The IB Diploma is not for everyone. Although it is a wonderfully challenging program that has gained incredible worldwide recognition, you need to look at your individual scenario and decide if the program is right for you and is beneficial to reaching your goals. I feel like some students are forced into the program by their parents and just have no motivation to work. If this sounds like you, then perhaps you should consider dropping out of the program.

NEW IB SCHOOLS

Newer programs may not quite have the curriculum organized effectively enough. Even an excellent teacher who's previously taught AP, for example, may for the first year find IAs and whatnot really tricky to wrap their head around. For a whole school to adopt the program, it's even tougher!

There are also lots of charter or even public schools that have all students take the diploma and exams whether or not they are ready for the level of academic rigor.

In fact, some schools don't offer the certificates program, so all students are required to take the full IB diploma. However, the percentage of kids willing and able to fight it out to the end is far lower.

It's no secret that the IBO has adopted a rather aggressive growth and marketing campaign to try and reach all the corners of the world and get more and more schools to adopt the IB Diploma program. As I am a strong believer in the program, I don't think this is much of a problem, however it does have some unfortunate consequences.

The most obvious one is that the newer schools are often less equipped to deal with the IB Diploma than the more established schools. The new schools offer fewer courses, and in general have less-experienced IB teachers. This usually results in a lower pass rate as the students are forced to teach themselves a lot of the IB specific stuff (like how to properly do IAs or IB examination techniques).

This book aims to fix that.

RESOURCE INEQUALITY

Related to the point above is the idea that not all schools share the same wealth of resources.

The private international schools are capable of wielding their financial strength to equip students with the best academic resources. A $120 examination paper and markscheme pack from the IBO store may not seem like much to private IB schools, however state sponsored educational establishments will struggle to get this kind of funding. This leads to an unlevel playing field as many IB students don't get a chance to see what past papers look like simply because their school can't afford it.

Don't believe me? Here's a little anecdote. In the November 2023 examinations, there were 179 students who achieved a maximum score of 45. Of those, 68 students came from just a couple of schools in Singapore.

Singapore's average IBDP score was 35.05 which surpasses the global average. The global average score was 30.24.

In Singapore, 409 students out of 1,894 achieved 40-plus points. Singapore's pass rate is 94.79%. The global pass rate is 79.35% (85.6% in May 2022).

How is it that a handful of schools are responsible for more than half of all the maximum marks? I think the answer is that they have the best resources, staff, and experience.

These things go a long way.

Or they are just really good at cheating (joke).

DITCH THE IB FEAR

Another key reason why so many students fail is because they go into the program already expecting that they will not succeed.

You need to throw away all your negative preconceptions and fears about the IB diploma and start believing in yourself.

No matter who you are and what kind of academic record you have had up to this point in your life, the IB diploma program is an opportunity for you to start anew.

I know students that have come from C grade averages to end up in the high 30s on their IB diploma. I myself was quite a high-school slacker and troublemaker until I realized that my IB grades could decide a large part of my near future.

The key here is that natural intelligence and 'book-smart' are not essential to achieving IB success. What is essential however is the willpower and self-belief that you can survive and succeed in the most academically intense high school degree program and come out with flying colors.

Consider your two-year IB experience as something of a sporting event. The final exams are the grand finale, and everything before is your preparation and training for that event. I use this sporting analogy because it highlights the importance of planning and mental preparedness that is needed to perform at the highest level. Even the greatest athletes cannot do their best unless they master the skill of visualizing their own success.

Without getting too philosophical, I do want to stress how important this 'visualization' exercise is. Unless you can imagine yourself getting the top marks and achieving a total of 40+ points, it will be very difficult to do so in reality. This is not a 'self-help' book per se, nor do I fully agree with the ideas that some self-help books tend to promote – most famously <u>The Secret</u>'s notion that anything is possible if you keep thinking about it. However, although I don't think that visualization alone is sufficient for success, I do think that it is necessary.

When someone tells you that the IB program is 'difficult', you need to appreciate that difficulty is always relative. Yes, perhaps compared to the A-Levels or the AP program, the IB is more academically challenging and there is more work to be done. However, this does not mean that the IB is the hardest task any 16–18-year-old kids across the world must face.

Trust me, there will be much more demanding and stressful challenges as you get older. Don't let this 'IB fear' become a scapegoat for underperformance. I see this happen all the time. Students get lost in this illusion of the IB as something impossible, and subsequently lose any motivation to do well because they think it is beyond their reach. This is where mental strength is of utmost importance.

The first few weeks of the IB program are relatively tranquil. Use this 'easing-in' period as an opportunity to prove to yourself that you can conquer and beat anything the IB program throws at you. Only once you overcome your mental fear of the IB program can you begin to deal with the challenges of the program itself.

It is imperative that your first few weeks of the program go as smoothly as possible. If you start to fall behind early, any preconceived fears you may have had will soon turn into a reality. So at least for the first month or so make sure you meet all of the deadlines and perform at your highest level.

Once you have proven to yourself that you can overcome the first month, any fear left will gradually dissolve.

MAKING THE MOST OF PRE-IB

Now that we've got the fear aspect out of the way, the question becomes: how should you best spend the few months leading up to your first day in the IB program? Unfortunately, there is no concrete answer, and you will hear a variety of responses when asking who has been through it all. However, there are certainly some things you can do that are more beneficial than others.

Summertime is here and you must relax, so for a few weeks forget that you are even in the IB. I suggest doing this at the start of summer. I also strongly recommend traveling and relaxing with friends and family. Take this as an opportunity to reset and go fresh into the IB next year. Now say 3-2 weeks are left before the IB starts or restarts, what do you do? You get back to work and you work hard! Ok, but what do you work on? Firstly, be sure that there is nothing you don't understand from the previous year. Make sure to patch up all your weak points. If there is something you don't understand in Chemistry, go over it, review it and then test yourself.

Do not be afraid to send a few emails to your teachers, they will find it incredible that you are working during your summer. If you have also noticed that you are not good at a particular type of assignment, for example you seem to score poorly on certain types of English essays, research them, rewrite a few essays and then ask your teacher to look over them.

23

Say you have patched up all your areas of weakness, what now? It's time to get ahead of the game. Look over the assignments you will have to do next year and start preparing for those. If you can't do that, then look over certain particularly difficult topics you will be doing next year and go over them. In all honesty you will probably not have much time to get ahead, most of your 2-3 weeks will be consumed with review work and patching any weakness in your knowledge. On that note, enjoy the summer and best of luck to you.

Disclaimer: if you are reading this section already well into your IB journey (say, summer of IBY1 to IBY2) – DO NOT STRESS OUT! You are not behind in any way, shape, or form. Only a small percentage of IB students actually get 'ahead of the game' and start to work on IB stuff before the start of IBY1. Most students who read this book are already a few months into their IB program, so do not worry about the past and instead focus on the present and the future!

24

CHAPTER 3

HOW TO DO THE BASICS

"You know you're in the IB when you can't explain how any of it works."

The IB program is a little bit different from any other high school curriculum. While there is a lot to learn, the IB is not focused on teaching facts and figures. Rather, the goal is to teach you **how to learn**.

Yes, as cliché as that sounds, you read that right. The International Baccalaureate Diploma Programme is not notoriously difficult because of the volume of information you need to know. While memorization, research, and writing dozens of papers is certainly not easy, this is not the most challenging part of the IB.

The most difficult aspect of the IB diploma is improving and changing your mindset about who you are, the way you go to school every day, and the way that you do your homework every night.

EVERYTHING YOU KNOW IS WRONG

I know that having to re-evaluate everything you know about how to go to school can feel like a slap in the face. However, the IB is only torture if you make it so. The program is difficult and demanding and even though many students give up every year, many more students actually receive their diploma.

The secret to beating the IB Diploma lies in your **attitude**.

If you are approaching the IB Diploma program this huge monster ready to swallow you up whole, then that is exactly what will happen to you if you are not careful. Soul, balls, and all. Change your attitude, however, and you will find the entire experience bearable, and dare I say, maybe even enjoyable.

The goal of the IB diploma program is to create students who think. Life-long learners who can look at problems in new and creative ways and use information to come to unique conclusions. This program is designed to create students who do not just know facts, but how to go out and dig up new answers.

By opening this book, you have already taken the initiative to become one of these students. Use this guide until the pages are ripped and torn.

> **Pro Tip:** The IB is not going to suck your life away. Now, repeat:
>
> THE IB IS NOT GOING TO SUCK MY LIFE AWAY.

This book is here to shape you into a super student – someone ready to tackle the world and take life head on.

PROFILE OF AN IB CANDIDATE

Before we can establish what you want out of the IB Diploma, it is important to know what the IB wants out of you. The International Baccalaureate Diploma programme is focused on developing students who are.

Inquirers	Principled
Critical Thinkers	Caring
Communicators	Open-minded
Risk Takers	Well-balanced
Knowledgeable	Reflective

I know that it sounds a bit like bullsh*t but do keep these traits in mind. Every learning objective in each IB course directly relates back to them. By mastering each trait, the diploma program will come naturally to you, and you will find yourself with less stress, more time, and better grades.

TWO PATHWAYS

There are two pathways for students who take IB classes: certificates or the full IB Diploma.

IB Certificates

The simplest option for students is the certificate program. Students can attend and test in their choice of IB courses and receive certificates in each respective subject. Schools have different requirements for taking these classes but for the most part, to take an IB class and receive a certificate simply means enrolling in the course and taking the appropriate exams.

The benefit of the certificate program is that you can take IB classes, but without any commitment beyond any particular course that you sign up for.

In most schools, a student who is only taking classes for certificates must still complete their school's state-mandated requirements in order to graduate.

> **Pro-Tip:** really ask yourself if the full IB Diploma is right for you. Perhaps you are being forced to take something that isn't a good fit and you would be better off taking certificates or enrolling in another program altogether.

IB Diploma

The other option for students is the full IB Diploma program. Students who attempt a full diploma complete classes in all areas of the IB program: including the Theory of Knowledge (TOK), Creativity, Activity and Service (CAS), and an Extended Essay project (EE).

In most schools, students must apply to get into the diploma program and are accepted by the school based on criteria that includes academic performance and their personal goals in the program. Requirements for admission are set at the discretion of the school and IB coordinator.

The focus of this book is on the full IB Diploma program. While the information here is still intrinsically valuable for any student, it is written mainly under the assumption that you are a *full diploma student*.

THE BILINGUAL DIPLOMA

This one is for the real achievers. Candidates who successfully complete courses in multiple languages are eligible to receive a bilingual diploma. Additionally, receiving a bilingual diploma allows candidates to take courses from groups 3 and 4 in a language that is not their first.

Bilingual diplomas are awarded for completing:

- Two Language A courses
- A group 3 or 4 subject taken in a language other than the candidates Language A
- An extended essay in a group 3 or group 4 subject written in a language other than the candidates Language A.

For further details, I highly recommend chasing down your IB coordinator (if your school could afford a competent one) and talking to them.

BENEFITS OF THE IB DIPLOMA

The International Baccalaureate program offers numerous benefits for diploma candidates.

The intangible benefits of the diploma program are countless. Going through the IB is basically boot camp training in how to critically think and reason. It is a crash course in academic excellence.

Attempting an IB diploma teaches you how to work under pressure as well as how to organize your thoughts, activities, and time during high school to a level that many people will not achieve during their entire lives.

The IB diploma has numerous tangible benefits as well. In my mind, this is the best college prep program out there. Many others, including top colleges and universities agree that the IB diploma is one of the best college prep programs in the world.

More and more, colleges and universities are recognizing the International Baccalaureate for developing intellectual, educated, motivated, and generally well-prepared students.

Many US and Canadian colleges will give credit based on a student's IB score. At some universities, students can earn up to what is equivalent to a year of college credit for their work in the IB Diploma.

A student going to an American university can expect to earn around 30 credits (equivalent to two-thirds of a year of study) towards their college degree before they even get the key to their dorm room. While some of your friends will have to take classes like English 101 during freshman year, you can party away or take some classes that actually interest you.

> **Pro Tip:** do not do the IB solely for the purpose of getting college credit – it is not worth the hassle and effort, and there has been a trend of awarding less and less credit so find out the specifics first.

Several of my classmates from IB have even used their credits to get out of college a year early, or to acquire two degrees in half the time that it takes most people.

Additionally, the IB program gives students the opportunity to attend university abroad. International schools are often hesitant to accept normal US high school grades because they see them as inconsistent and unreliable. The IB Diploma, however, is internationally recognized and can offer a reliable gateway to attending top schools outside of your home country.

ELEMENTS OF THE INTERNATIONAL BACCALAUREATE

From the outside, the IB Diploma program can seem to be inherently complicated, confusing and downright intimidating. For most of my IB career I had a very fuzzy picture of how the program actually worked.

Never knowing why something was happening, or what was going to be due when I was often stumbling blindly through course after course.

Many students want to know: why does the IB program have to be so f*cking complex? Well, the answer is that the IB is designed to be complete. When you understand the program as a whole, it becomes much easier to see where each piece fits.

STRUCTURE OF THE DIPLOMA PROGRAM

The diploma program is made up of six subjects. In order to receive an IB diploma, candidates must successfully complete one course in each subject area. The exception is the arts, as one can choose to take an additional course from another group (e.g. two sciences) instead of a group 6 class.

> Group 1: Studies in Language and Literature (Primary Language)

Group 2: Language Acquisition (Secondary Language)

Group 3: Study of Individuals and Society

Group 4: Sciences

Group 5: Mathematics

Group 6: The Arts

Additionally, all candidates for the IB Diploma are required to:

- Submit an extended essay in one of the IB subject groups.
- Complete the course in Theory of Knowledge
- Fulfill requirements for CAS.

CLASSES AND ASSESSMENT

Each course in the diploma program is structured around a common curriculum. While the given curriculum for some courses is completer and more specific than others, each one includes a list of topics that are expected to be covered as well as learning objectives for each subject.

Beyond this, IB teachers are specifically trained to develop and implement courses according to standards and requirements set out by the IBO.

This means that while the exact course curriculum may vary from school to school, around the globe, IB courses are basically the same.

One of the key differences between IB and normal high school is how courses are graded. Scoring for IB courses relies solely on assessment. That is, assignments and homework do not count towards receiving an IB diploma (this is a crucial aspect that we will address in detail in the chapter on Internal Assessment).

IB courses are graded based on two types of assessments: internal and external. Generally, a course will have one internal assessment project and one two- or three-part external assessment.

Internal Assessments

These are assignments, projects, or portfolios that reflect work done during a class.

The internal assessment is graded by the course instructor who evaluates the work according to requirements set up by the IBO. After the assessments for the course are graded, the instructor will send their grades along with several samples of the work from the class to the IBO.

Trained and impartial evaluators then re-grade the sample work and adjust the scores for the entire class accordingly.

This means that while the course instructor grades internal assessments, the IB moderates this grading so that any errors or bias in an instructor's grading can be adjusted for.

External Assessments

The external assessment is an exam which covers every section of the curriculum and takes place at the end of the course. In the Northern Hemisphere, IB exams take place over a period of several weeks in May.

In the Southern Hemisphere, IB schools conduct their exams in November.

Each external assessment is composed of several 'papers' or sections of the exam, which test different sections of the course. Each paper contains questions in one of several different formats.

The time given to complete each paper can vary from 45 minutes to more than 2 hours. The papers for a single subject may be tested over multiple days giving students time to prepare for each specific paper in advance.

The external assessment is administered at the school and all completed papers are sent to various locations around the globe to be officially evaluated by the IB.

These assignments are heavily standardized and the IB expects that every student in each IB school around the world will take the exact same version of a respective exam.

For a strange example, one of my friends took his HL chemistry exam without a periodic table of elements because one school in India did not receive copies in time for their examination and tested without the table.

As they didn't get the periodic table for their exam, neither did my friend! You can imagine the outrage that occurred...

GRADES

IB courses are graded on a scale of 1-7. Each grade is a combination of the scores from the external and internal assessments. The weight each assessment carries may vary depending on the course.

The standards for grading in the IB are different from those used in the majority of schools.

They are intensively quantitative, and each course is graded on an exact and strict mark scheme.

Grades are assigned on a scale from 1-7:

> 7 Excellent performance
>
> 6 Very good performance
>
> 5 Good performance
>
> 4 Satisfactory performance
>
> 3 Mediocre performance
>
> 2 Poor performance
>
> 1 Very poor performance

On a more quantitative level, each question carries a certain number of points.

Each exam is then scored out of this total number of possible points. So, in effect, a score of 7 is roughly equivalent to a 100 percent, a score of 5 equivalent to 80 percent, etc.

TOK and the Extended Essay are graded on a scale of A-E

> A Excellent performance
>
> B Good performance
>
> C Satisfactory performance
>
> D Mediocre performance
>
> E Elementary performance

In many North American schools, only an A or B is seen as acceptable marks and students are graded on the idea that good work deserves an A.

The IB, however, grades on philosophy that 'good' work is average – and thus merits at most C or B. In most cases, only excellent work will receive a B while a piece must be truly outstanding to merit an A.

To this end, scoring a 7 on an exam or an A or on your Extended Essay is not common and scoring this high is a sign that you have greatly exceeded expectations for the assignment.

CONTENT

Even though IB courses are evaluated by examination, the curriculum takes deliberate steps to ensure that the course is not taught solely 'for the exam'.

You will still receive homework and grades for your classes that are required for your regular high school diploma.

It is still somewhat important to do daily homework.

Not only will homework ensure that you pass high school, but it is also an essential tool to prepare for your IB exams.

HL/ SL COURSES

Each IB course is offered at one of two levels: Higher Level (HL) or Standard Level (SL).

Of the courses studied in the IB, three to four must be completed at the Higher Level (HL) of study, and no more than three courses may be completed at the Standard Level (SL) way of study.

HL and SL courses differ in three major ways:

1. First, HL courses are taught over significantly more time than SL courses. Each HL course is allotted 240 teaching hours while an SL course is allotted 150 hours. This means that, in some schools, HL courses are taught over two years while SL courses take place in one. However, some schools opt to teach both courses over two years, spending extra classes and free periods on HL courses.

2. The second major difference lies in the extra depth and detail that is covered by HL courses. Due to there being much more time to learn the subject, HL courses explore their subjects at greater depth and with additional topics when compared to the SL courses. To this end, students in an HL course are expected to develop higher level skills in a particular topic than students in an equivalent SL course.

3. The third major difference between HL and SL courses is reflected in the course assessments. External assessments at the HL level often include additional papers to cover the extra material, and the papers themselves tend to be longer and more in-depth than SL papers. While the requirements for the internal assessments tend to be the same for both HL and SL course levels, the internal assessments from HL classes are graded with the expectation that students understand the material and the assignment at a higher level.

Pro Tip: when deciding whether to take a class at SL or HL, take a careful look at the differences in the syllabus. For certain classes, such as economics, it might actually be helpful to take HL to gain a better understanding of the material. On the other hand, most science courses have significant differences in the volume and difficulty of material covered in HL as opposed to SL.

TIMELINE

The Pre-IB

Depending on your school, there may or may not be a pre-IB program offered. If there is, the first step of your IB career will probably be taking those pre-IB classes. The IB Diploma is officially a two-year program, however, due to its rigor and complexity, many schools elect to ease students into the program with advanced 'IB-like' courses during the first two years before starting IB.

The pre-IB program gives you an opportunity to get used to the higher level of classwork demanded in the IB before you commit to the full diploma program.

If you have taken advanced or honors classes before high school, the pre-IB won't be very different. The two years in pre-IB give you a chance to get to know the IB teachers at your school, take classes in a more challenging environment and to see if you really want to attempt an IB diploma.

For many students the pre-IB is the best time to get used to more challenging courses and to figure out a game plan for their years in the diploma program. In the time before you start the diploma, the best thing to do is to begin adapting our schedule to focus on school. Do not forget the rest of your life; just try to invest more time in your studies and classes than you did previously.

Do not just complete assignments and write papers; Wikipedia or Google search what you are learning about to get a complete picture of the subject. Do the bonus problems at the back of your math chapters and go to your local library to look up topics that you learn about in other subjects.

While having this little extra knowledge and going the extra distance is not required to pass classes in the pre-IB, the IB diploma program is structured around students who go the extra mile in their studies.

Your teachers will be looking for this in Pre-IB and even more so once you enter the full diploma program. Set yourself up early for success and you will find it much easier to overcome the many difficulties that IB students face.

IB Year 1

Your first year in the IB will probably be the 'easier' one. You start your HL classes this year and (depending on your school) start and possibly finish your SL classes. At the end of the year, you may have the opportunity to take examinations for your SL classes to get them out of the way. In the second half of the year, you usually start TOK and you need to start work on your Extended Essay. If your school is lenient, I would recommend getting a head-start on your EE, and starting the second year with <u>at least</u> a solid, detailed outline. Ideally, you should try and finish your EE in your first year, as the first semester of the second year is usually the most chaotic and stressful one, with all the IAs piling up on top of your usual classwork.

IB Year 2

Over the summer and into your final year in IB, you will continue to work on your Extended Essay, finishing sometime around December or January. You will finish TOK around the same time and all your CAS requirements must be completed before testing at the end of the year. Having to test in 3-4 HL courses as well as 2-3 SL courses makes this the hardest year in IB.

CHAPTER 4

HOW TO CHOOSE YOUR SUBJECTS

Two roads diverged in a yellow wood,
And sorry I could not travel both
And be one traveler, long I stood
And looked down one as far as I could
To where it bent in the undergrowth;

Then took the other, as just as fair,
And having perhaps the better claim,
Because it was grassy and wanted wear;
Though as for that the passing there
Had worn them really about the same,

And both that morning equally lay
In leaves no step had trodden black.
Oh, I kept the first for another day!
Yet knowing how way leads on to way,
I doubted if I should ever come back.

I shall be telling this with a sigh
Somewhere ages and ages hence:
Two roads diverged in a wood, and I—
I took the one less travelled by,
And that has made all the difference.

- *Robert Frost*

I wanted to start this extremely important chapter with one of my favorite poems. The meaning and interpretation of this poem has always been the subject of great debate, but to me, this poem is all about the fragility and importance of decision making.

How does this relate to IB subject choice? Well, simply put, choosing the wrong subjects can make the difference between getting your IB Diploma or not, or getting that perfect 45 or not.

For example, I am still convinced – nay, adamant – that had I chosen Biology instead of Physics, I would be sitting here and telling you all about my perfect score of 45. It's that simple. When I saw what Biology entailed and had a look at the statistics for getting 7's as well as what required in terms of memorization, it became clear that choosing Biology would have 100% been the smarter choice (especially since Physics was not required for any of my post-IB stuff).

Every school has a unique stance in which courses they offer for each subject group. Many schools will offer just one or two classes in each subject area, while larger richer schools may offer more choice. It is important to remember that the IB program at every school is unique, and that some, if not many of the course options described here may not be available at your school. Like the rest of this book, use this section as a reference tool and not a definitive guide.

While many of the courses in the diploma are similar, every course has its unique quirks and characteristics. If you need details about a particular course or subject area, speak to your program coordinator or the teacher at your school that instructs in that particular course.

Although to many of you this chapter will have little relevance, to those who are yet to decide which subjects you want to take – this chapter is of great importance. I find that choosing your subjects is, rather unfortunately, underestimated in importance.

You are deciding what you will learn in depth for the next two years of your life. So, just as you would take time to choose a college degree, an occupation or a spouse, you should sit down and think about what you want and, more importantly, what will maximize your chances of convincingly passing and getting the highest possible grades. There are a few factors that you should consider, and I have outlined these below:

INTEREST

As with almost everything you do, you will tend to succeed more and find it easier if you are doing something you have an interest in and enjoy. The same goes for IB subjects. Although this is of less importance in choosing a group 1 or 2 language, it has great importance in choosing your group 4 science and group 3 subject.

If you know for a fact that you have absolutely no passion and interest for memorizing human anatomy and studying Biology, then you can cross that off. If, on the other hand, you want your IB to have as little mathematics as possible, then you probably would not be too interested in studying Physics. If you are strongly passionate about a certain subject and are already reading external material concerned with it, then by all means go ahead and take it into consideration.

However, one should be careful not to confuse interest with vague curiosity. If you always thought that graffiti is cool, it would not be wise choosing HL Visual Art solely based on that observation. Similarly, don't let a childhood obsession with spaceships be the deciding factor for choosing HL Physics. This is where a slight familiarity with the course content can greatly help. Take the time to glance over the syllabus of the course you are interested in, and only then check to see if it matches your interests.

> **Pro Tip:** the course syllabus for every subject is available online via a quick google search. These documents are basically a rundown of everything you will be learning about on that course. Make sure you consult these when picking subjects.

ABILITY

Obviously if you are clearly naturally gifted in a certain subject then you should thank your natural abilities and take it. Of course, there are limitations to this rule of thumb. I used to be obsessed with drawing and graphic design, and for many years believed I would be studying Art at Diploma level.

However, as the time came for me to make my final decision, I did a little research and talked to many seniors who had previously done Art as a subject. The general feeling seemed to be that if I wanted to go for a subject that I enjoyed, excelled at, and wouldn't be under too much stress then I should choose Art instead of another Group 3 topic. Having done that research also showed me that it seemed very few get 7s in Art (especially in my school), no matter how passionate or how good the candidate is (perhaps due to the nature of the final exam and luck of the draw). Granted, there are some schools that excel at getting their kids high Art grades.

Since I was more concerned with obtaining a 7 than following my passion for Art and gambling with the grade, I chose geography (which I also had a reasonable ability for).

The message I am trying to get across is that often students get confused about how great their abilities are in a certain subject. Just because you got As in English in middle school does not mean that you should expect to jump into a Higher-Level English exam and effortlessly produce a grade 7 piece of work. Be honest with yourself when assessing your own ability in a certain subject.

FUTURE

Please don't get me wrong. When I say future I don't mean that the subjects you choose for your IB diploma will reflect in any way where you will be in ten years and what sort of occupation you will have (although, funnily enough, they have for me).

Nevertheless, you do need to take into consideration what you want to do at university level if you plan on pursuing a university education. It's unfortunate that you need to be thinking about your post-school decision from almost the age of 16 when university is probably the last thing on your mind but that's the reality of it.

All too often I have seen students wanting to study medicine at a top UK university be rejected because, despite taking Biology as a subject, they did not take Chemistry, which is often a requirement to study medical science. The same can be said for students wanting to study Economics. Taking the wrong kind of math course severely limits your chances of ending up on a top Economics course – in most cases.

Thus, if you're one of those students that has his/her heart set on a specific course at a specific university by the age of 16, then you should do some research and find out which courses are essential, and which will help you in getting closer to your goal. For those of you thinking of studying abroad, you may want to reconsider which foreign languages you want to take, if your school offers a wider variety.

Although this is important to take into consideration, don't worry *too much* about it. In most cases offers from universities are given based on a final score, rather than subject-specific. Also, I have seen people go on to get PhDs in Economics without having taken Economics as an IB subject. So, with regards to the long-term future, subject choice is probably not the most important factor to consider.

TEACHERS

This is a tough one. I hate to say it but there is such a thing as a "bad teacher" even in the glamorous top-of-the-line world of the IB Diploma. Trust me; I have seen the best of both worlds. Some of the teachers I have worked with were masters at what they did, with more than a decade of first-hand IB experience. Then there were those who probably couldn't spell International Baccalaureate – let alone teach it. Most students tend to believe this idea where the teacher is the one factor that will make or break the subject. They think that the teacher has a greater influence on the final grade than they do themselves.

I do not agree. Even if your teacher is utterly useless at what they are hired to do, this does not mean you should spend two years moaning only to ultimately fail the subject and live your whole life cursing that teacher.

Believe me, I have seen some of the worst of the worst. But even despite the poor teaching I've seen students get past that and take matters into their own hands to achieve a grade they truly deserve.

Yes, it's true, if you have a poor teacher then you will spend most of your time becoming best friends with the subject textbooks. But let's be honest here, we don't live in a perfect world, hence we don't all have world class IB teachers.

With regards to the subject material, you should not have to worry too much if your teacher is clueless. But, when it comes to things such as sending off internal assessments and choosing options for examinations, you should ensure that they know what they are talking about. You don't want to sit a two-year program only to find that your teacher messed up the internal assessments you gave in and thus you lose almost 25% of your total mark.

By the time you begin your IB program, you will have heard all the rumors about who is a great IB teacher and who shouldn't even be teaching preschool. Don't completely ignore these. If you're the type of person who simply cannot take matters into their own hands and work independently for most of the year, then by all means look for the "best" and most engaging teachers that are available. If, on the other hand, you don't need to be spoon-fed information that is readily available for you yourself to read from the textbooks, then it shouldn't matter. In this case, you should choose subjects based on the other criteria I have outlined.

> **Pro Tip:** before you start the IBDP, go and talk to your potential teachers and ask them about the courses. By talking to them you will get a much better picture of what life will be like in their class.

If you thought that those were the only factors to consider when choosing your courses, well you would be mistaken. The top students also consider some less obvious elements.

SCHOOL RECORDS

If you are one of those students taking the IB Diploma simply to obtain the highest score possible no matter which subjects then you would be wise to do a little bit of research. Find out how well your school has performed in different subjects over the years. If for the past ten years not a single person has gotten a 7 in Chemistry, then your best bet would probably be not to choose it if you are looking for a 7 in your Group 4 subject. If on the other hand, it has been decades since someone has gotten below a 5 in your school's History SL program, and you are the type of person that would be more than happy with a 5 or above then by all means go for it.

Don't limit this research to your school records alone. Go online and find out which subjects have the greatest fail rates, the greatest number of 7's, and what the median marks are. All of this information is readily available on the IBO website – under the section of 'Statistical Bulletins' (we will revisit these in greater detail at the end of the chapter).

There is an abundance of information in these reports, so take the time to analyze them. I don't encourage making decisions completely based on statistics but playing the numbers game will not prevent you from making better choices.

DIFFICULTY

There is a myth in the IB world that claims that all IB kids do an equal amount of work, no matter what subjects they choose. Perhaps the phrasing is a bit unclear there. Yes, it can be that the actual amount of work (hours assigned) is the same from subject to subject. Don't be fooled into thinking that each candidate faces the same difficulty. This is especially true because of the IB's system of separating Higher Level and Standard Level subjects.

Take two random students with exactly the same subject choices, apart from the fact that student X takes Math AA HL and Geography SL, whereas student Y takes Math AI SL and Geography HL.

One would have an incredibly difficult time arguing that the gap in difficulty between Math AI SL and AA HL is the same as the gap between Geography SL and HL. The gap in difficulty between Math AA HL and AI SL is incomparable to the gap in Geography.

There is no point in kidding ourselves. If you want to challenge yourself, then by all means take HL: Economics, Mathematics, English, Physics, SL: History, Language B.

If you want to lay back a bit and not be under too much stress and get a guaranteed pass, take HL: Theatre Arts, Geography, Environmental Systems and Societies, SL: English, Language (ab initio), and Business Management.

Let's be honest here; it's no secret that Physics or Chemistry are academically more demanding than Environmental Systems and Societies. However, I must warn you, don't fall into a trap thinking Visual Arts is an easy course: in M23 it was the class with the least amounts of 7's! Do careful research to discover which courses are usually considered "easier", both at your school and globally.

All of this is not something to be ashamed of either. You may opt to take a less stressful route, with a lighter workload – and this is perfectly fine. The point I am trying to make is that you need to figure out what your ultimate aim is.

Do you want to choose demanding courses that interest you and will challenge you? Or do you have little interest in what subjects you do as long as you get 35+ by the end of the two years? There is little wrong with either of the choices, but the important thing to remember is that the choice is real, and the choice is yours.

RESOURCES

As much as the IB tries to make their students more educated, inquisitive and imaginative, I am often shocked at how little students use the resources available at their disposal.

The Internet is an invaluable weapon in your IB survival toolkit. Go online and find out if there are any great books available on your subjects of interest. Find out how long the course has been taught and whether it has been significantly modified in recent years.

Keep in mind that if the resources are scarce for your subject of interest, then it probably means that you will struggle to find help outside your classroom.

More well-established subjects have an incredible surplus of information readily available to find on the internet and in books. The newer subjects, or the less popular choices, will undoubtedly have less helpful information.

Pro Tip: hop online and check what kind of resources are available for your courses. This includes textbooks and IB resources.

WHAT IF THE SUBJECT I WANT IS NOT AVAILABLE?

I fully appreciate that there are many students out there crying "my school just launched the IB Diploma program and I don't have a choice of what science to choose because they only offer Chemistry at HL!" Unfortunately, that is just a fact of life. Not a single school will offer all the IB subject choices that are available, so you need to make the best out of the situation. Don't waste your time protesting and making petitions asking your school to introduce a subject that would probably yield high demand from the students. It's much more complicated than that as there are monetary, time and faculty constraints that need to be considered.

In certain specific circumstances, however, there are ways in which you can 'create' a new subject for yourself – given your school allows this. You could potentially sit the two years in a HL class only to then take the SL exam. This may be frowned upon by your school but try to see if this is possible. I initially started the IB program with the intention of doing four HL subjects (Economics, Mathematics, Geography and Physics) as opposed to the usual three. However, as the time came to make final exam choices, I realized that I would be better off dropping one of my HLs rather than risking getting a lower grade. Physics HL was unfortunately a bit too demanding for me, and I argued that it took away too much revision time from my other HL subjects in which I was trying to achieve 7s. I repeatedly asked the IB coordinator to be allowed to sit the SL Physics exam and continue to sit the Physics HL class. Eventually all the details were sorted out and it worked out fine.

I'm not saying sit HL classes for all of your subjects, but this is certainly an overlooked tactic for the more ambitious students out there. If you are not challenged enough and would find it beneficial learning some HL material despite sitting the SL exam then try to make that possible by carefully discussing it with your IB coordinator. Note also that the HL teacher may be much 'better' than the SL one.

There is also the possibility of self-study or following online courses (check the Pamoja online education program). Again, you will need to check this with your school and IB coordinator. It is understandable why many schools are wary of external course providers. Also, there is a monetary burden to consider.

At the end of the day the choice of which subjects you will do will largely depend on how the schedule blocks your schoolwork and what subjects they actually have on offer. Don't make a huge fuss if you can't get exactly what you want. There are thousands of students out there in similar situations – if not worse. Work with what you have. Take my tips listed above, consult your parents, consult your teachers, consult your older school friends and hopefully this will help you reach a decision.

Do not choose a subject "because my friend is doing it as well." This is probably the dumbest thing you can do when it comes to making subject choices. Chances are you and your "friends" will see each other in other classes, and you'll have enough time to hang out outside of class.

ANTICIPATED SUBJECT

An 'Anticipated' subject is just the IB's fancy name for an accelerated subject. When you sign up to study an Anticipated subject, you have about one year to actually finish the entire subject. This means that you will have only 5 subjects to worry about in the last year of IB. But this also means a lot more stress during the first year of IB when you have to cram two years of content into just one year.

Most people's first reaction is something like: what if I can't physically learn that much content in just one year!? My advice for dispelling the anxiety: at my school, everyone (i.e., 150 of us) did one Anticipated subject. Some schools even allow people to take 2 Anticipated subjects. Achieving a grade 7 in Anticipated is also very feasible. So, don't worry, the workload is doable.

You can only choose SL subjects to Anticipate. Most subjects are great to Anticipate, but I would personally stay away from the more notorious Anticipated subjects. History is already infamously difficult as a two-year course. I personally wouldn't select it as an Anticipated subject. English A Literature or Lang Lit – a very small number of 7s for the two-year course, so I wouldn't bet on getting a 7 in Anticipated. Mathematics – university admissions tend to require at least two years of senior Mathematics. However, Mathematics is one of those courses that works well with

Anticipated. Mathematics is more about practice and I think you can pick up math skills quickly. Second language subjects are fantastic to Anticipate if you are already somewhat proficient in the language.

I would advise most people to Anticipate a Group 3 Humanities subject (apart from History, of course!):

Psychology – a lot of people at my school did this. It worked great for me, but Psychology is a lot of rote learning and material. It's not an easy ride by any means, but it is probably more manageable than History.

Business and Management – even more people at my school anticipated B&M. Many people have the impression that it's an 'easy' subject, but I can't say anything on the topic because I've never done it. In the end, all subjects take time and commitment. Choosing the right anticipated subject is about knowing your strengths and considering the costs and benefits for you personally.

Doing an Anticipated subject is a good way to minimize stress and sleep deprivation in your second year of IB, with the trade-off being a slightly greater workload during your first year. You experience a real IB exam before you do all your other exams in final year. I found that the familiarity with the exam procedure really helped with nerves and pre-exam anxiety.

STATISTICS: LET'S CHOOSE YOUR SUBJECTS

Okay, now that we have discussed all the important factors, it's time to choose your subjects. But before we do, there is one more factor we need to consider – and it's something that I have mentioned previously in this chapter. We need to look at the IBO statistical bulletin and see which subjects are fail traps, which subjects have the best average points total, and which subjects are an easy ride to a 7.

In the following section I am going to go over each group and the individual subject statistics. I am going to recommend a course for each group; however, this recommendation is only based on the statistical benefit that subject will bring to *succeeding/passing the IB* (as the book title suggests). If you wish to maximize your IB mark, then this is not the same as maximizing the chance of passing.

I would also like to stress taking a subject you are genuinely interested in, or that you are willing to dedicate more time to is obviously a better choice than anything statistics could dictate. As important as passing the IB is, it will be made a bit easier if you are doing something you enjoy. That being said, don't take this next section for granted: taking into account the global passing rates can make or break your IB experience.

GROUP 1

Although you can access the statistics for Language Acquisition in the latest IBO statistical bulletin, I don't think it will be that much help:

Subject	Candidates	Mean Grade	% 1	% 2	% 3	% 4	% 5	% 6	% 7
ENGLISH A LAL HL	37,267	4.79	0.0	0.9	9.2	29.8	33.9	22.3	3.8
ENGLISH A LAL SL	24,851	4.88	0.0	0.7	7.0	29.3	34.2	24.2	4.6
ENGLISH A LIT HL	30,680	4.56	0.0	1.4	8.6	38.8	35.4	14.7	1.0
ENGLISH A LIT SL	5,700	4.91	0.0	0.5	6.6	25.2	40.5	23.1	3.9

source: https://www.ibo.org/globalassets/new-structure/about-the-ib/pdfs/dp-cp-provisional-statistical-bulletin-may-2023.pdf

There is a strong belief that Language and Literature (LAL) is easier and less time consuming than Literature (LIT). This is generally true. Thus, if you really like literature and analysis, and are willing to dedicate more time to this class, then stick with Lit, but otherwise go for LAL as it will be **much** less work.

The percentages for people getting a 7 are not great for any of the subjects, with only 2 to 5 students out of every hundred getting that maximum mark.

Basically, for you, the choice needs to be taking your best language as a group 1 subject – and most probably taking it at SL.

I would only recommend taking Language and Literature as an HL if that is really where you excel and what you plan to study further on. Or, if you are very desperate for an HL subject.

It's still interesting to note how few (less than 3%) get a 7 in HL Literature. Based on those mean grades, it does look as if English A Language and Literature SL is the most appealing choice.

Also note how the mean grades are significantly lower for the HL courses than the SL courses. I attribute this mostly to a lot of kids taking it at HL thinking they are very good at it (because of previous success in high school literature classes) when really they are not.

Of course, if English isn't your first language or if you are much better versed in your mother tongue, you can look into those statistics as well – but I am not going to reproduce all of them here.

Recommendation: English A Language and Literature SL

GROUP 2

Okay so now it's time to decide which language you are going to 'learn'. I put learn in quotation marks because the smartest thing you can do here, if you are a non-English speaker (but chose English as Group 1 subject), is to just choose your mother tongue as a language B.

Here's just a sample of some of the stats from the M23 examinations:

Subject	Candidates	Mean Grade	% 1	% 2	% 3	% 4	% 5	% 6	% 7
RUSSIAN AB. SL	65	5.31		9.4	3.1	15.6	21.9	18.8	31.3
RUSSIAN B HL	88	6.44				2.3	6.8	35.2	55.7
RUSSIAN B SL	117	5.96			1.8	7.9	24.6	24.6	41.2
JAPANESE AB. SL	438	4.73	0.9	8.3	14.4	19.4	22.9	18.5	15.5
JAPANESE B HL	116	6.30		5.2	1.7	2.6	5.2	18.3	67.0

source: https://www.ibo.org/globalassets/new-structure/about-the-ib/pdfs/dp-cp-provisional-statistical-bulletin-may-2023.pdf

Look at those mean grades and the amount of kids getting 7's. It's ridiculous.

Yes, this does seem 'unfair' to the other kids and there might be some diploma coordinators who try to kick up a fuss (hey, there are some kids who do this and choose their mother tongue as Ab Initio). However, you just need to convince them that ultimately the goal is to get the best grade possible. There's nothing stopping you from taking a language that you are proficient in as a language B. That's the smart thing to do.

Compare this to kids who challenge themselves and do French or German as a foreign language:

FRENCH AB. SL	4,753	4.78	0.3	3.9	15.7	19.5	28.4	22.4	9.8
FRENCH B HL	3,464	5.15	0.1	3.3	11.3	15.5	22.7	30.4	16.7
FRENCH B SL	11,935	5.02	0.0	2.3	9.6	21.5	29.3	24.6	12.6
GERMAN AB. SL	1,334	5.00		2.4	11.1	19.7	28.3	28.1	10.3
GERMAN B HL	1,667	5.67	0.3	2.7	10.1	25.3	40.0	21.7
GERMAN B SL	2,035	5.11		0.7	8.9	24.7	24.5	27.6	13.7

source: https://www.ibo.org/globalassets/new-structure/about-the-ib/pdfs/dp-cp-provisional-statistical-bulletin-may-2023.pdf

These are no longer native speakers – and as a result those average grades drop and only 10-20% get 7's.

Another important factor: if you take this subject as an SL – you can get it out of the way in the first year. Imagine that, not having to worry about speaking a 'foreign' language for the entirety of your IBY2…

If you can't do this for some reason, then I would recommend choosing a language at B that has the best teacher in your school. Teachers are rather important when learning a new language, so try to pick wisely. Also, choose one that doesn't hate you as they will be assessing the oral component which counts for quite a lot.

What about Ab Initio? Don't fall into the trap of believing Ab initio will be an easy class: it is arguably one of the most difficult language acquisition courses, especially if you are completely new to the language you are going to learn. I would recommend steering clear unless there is a language that you really want to learn for the future.

Recommendation: your (native) Language B (SL)

GROUP 3

Oh, the humanities! But unlike the Hindenburg, your experience in a group does not have to be a total disaster. Let's have a look at some stats from the previous examination session:

Subject	Candidates	Mean Grade	% 1	% 2	% 3	% 4	% 5	% 6	% 7
ART HISTORY SL	156	4.31	4.2	11.3	18.3	22.5	15.5	15.5	12.7
BRAZ.SOC.STUD SL	333	4.90	0.3	4.3	8.0	24.8	30.3	20.2	12.2
BUS MAN HL	19,220	4.94	0.2	3.4	8.9	21.2	30.6	27.3	8.3
BUS MAN SL	10,874	4.94	0.3	3.9	10.8	20.1	28.3	24.6	12.1
CL.GK.ROM.ST. SL	36	6.25				2.8	8.3	50.0	38.9
ECONOMICS HL	17,603	5.11	0.2	2.8	8.0	18.3	30.6	26.1	14.0
ECONOMICS SL	9,707	4.75	0.6	4.5	15.7	21.8	25.1	20.8	11.6
GEOGRAPHY HL	4,714	5.25	0.0	0.6	6.2	17.6	31.6	30.5	13.3
GEOGRAPHY SL	4,281	4.81	0.3	3.5	15.3	19.5	28.6	23.1	9.7
GLOB. POL HL	4,707	5.11		1.1	4.8	19.5	37.9	30.2	6.5
GLOB. POL SL	3,152	4.81		2.9	11.8	22.0	34.6	21.5	7.2
HISTORY HL	37,071	4.33	0.7	6.6	14.6	33.4	29.3	13.0	2.6
HISTORY SL	8,648	4.65	0.5	3.8	9.0	28.8	36.0	18.6	3.4
ITGS HL	1,141	4.30	0.7	1.7	18.5	36.5	31.6	10.2	0.8
ITGS SL	1,134	4.21	1.2	7.9	17.7	30.9	26.8	15.1	0.4
PHILOSOPHY HL	1,868	4.98		0.9	8.9	23.8	31.8	26.6	8.1
PHILOSOPHY SL	2,532	4.87	0.2	2.5	10.0	23.9	31.5	24.4	7.5
POLITICAL TH. SL	16	4.67		6.7	6.7	33.3	26.7	20.0	6.7
PSYCHOLOGY HL	14,013	4.78	0.2	2.8	11.6	25.2	29.3	25.8	5.1
PSYCHOLOGY SL	12,738	4.45	1.1	7.9	14.1	26.7	26.2	19.5	4.5
SOC.CUL.ANTH. HL	950	4.94	0.4	2.3	11.6	23.5	26.2	23.4	12.7
SOC.CUL.ANTH. SL	1,735	4.77		2.4	11.2	25.1	33.3	23.4	4.5
TURK 20TH CEN SL	738	5.22			4.6	22.8	29.9	31.2	11.5
WLD ART CULT SL	50	5.12			4.0	24.0	40.0	20.0	12.0
WORLD RELIG. SL	1,676	4.69	0.1	1.7	12.6	29.2	33.2	17.6	5.6

source: https://www.ibo.org/globalassets/new-structure/about-the-ib/pdfs/dp-cp-provisional-statistical-bulletin-may-2023.pdf

What sticks out for you? Those high percentages of 7s in Geography and Economics, that's for sure, as highlighted. Also, the 'new' subjects have a pretty decent mean grade, and not many people fail. It is important to note that a course such as CL.GK.Rom.St only has a high mean grade because a mere **36** people take it.

Full disclosure: I'm not a huge fan of these courses they keep adding. While I'm sure that Art History is a respectable course in its own right, I don't think it should be an IB subject because I don't think it has the same academic rigor as say, Economics. But that's not my place to judge.

My advice is to choose one or two of the 'classic' group 3 subjects, and to do them at HL. So, basically, a choice between: Business and Management, Economics, Geography, History, Psychology or Philosophy...

The only reason I recommend those more established courses is because you will have more resources at your disposal and also the teachers *tend* to be better.

Do not take this advice as definitive – if your heart is set on Brazilian Social Studies SL then by all means, good luck.

Be wary of choosing History – it is a LOT of memorization and a lot of writing. Some consider it the most difficult group 3 HL class. Students often complain about their workloads, especially at HL. I'd go for Economics HL instead if you have an interest in that.

So why both at HL?

Because you need to do 3 HL's and the group 3 gap between HL and SL is not that big compared to say, the difference between SL and HL Math.

> **Pro Tip:** check the syllabus for HL Econ and SL Econ – you won't find much of a gap. Meanwhile, HL History is nearly twice as much material as SL History..

Yes, the workload in HL is bigger, and you learn a bit more stuff, but I think if you can take the course as an HL – then do it. I am personally also of the opinion that for some courses, like economics, it is easier to take the class at HL. This is because the extra content covered strengthens your understanding of the SL content and allows you to perform better in IAs as well as analytical essays. There will be a lot of essay writing, and your hands might bleed when it comes time to write the exams (especially history students), but I think it's worth it.

Business and Management gets a lot of love on IB subject discussion threads. It seems that the course is 'easy' and very enjoyable. Also, there is a trend of students taking more business-oriented courses so they can study 'business' at university.

I did Econ and Geo and I loved both of them. If my school offered Philosophy I probably would have considered that too. History is also really appealing, but I just wasn't that interested in it at the time.

Recommendation: take TWO subjects of your choice and as HL's – preferably two that have been around for a while.

GROUP 4

Now let's move onto the dreaded Sciences:

Subject	Candidates	Mean Grade	% 1	% 2	% 3	% 4	% 5	% 6	% 7
ASTRONOMY SL	37	4.39		12.1	9.1	33.3	30.3	3.0	12.1
BIOLOGY HL	31,912	4.39	1.1	7.1	18.1	27.2	24.0	16.5	6.0
BIOLOGY SL	20,866	4.15	1.8	10.3	22.9	25.0	21.5	13.3	5.2
CHEMISTRY HL	17,100	4.56	1.3	8.3	16.1	21.4	23.4	18.9	10.5
CHEMISTRY SL	15,801	4.10	2.6	14.9	21.4	21.1	18.7	14.2	7.1
COMPUTER SC. HL	3,766	4.41	1.5	9.2	17.4	23.5	22.8	18.2	7.5
COMPUTER SC. SL	3,397	3.93	3.0	16.3	23.4	21.1	18.5	12.7	4.9
DESIGN TECH. HL	1,639	4.66	0.1	3.1	12.6	27.2	33.1	19.5	4.3
DESIGN TECH. SL	1,544	3.97	0.7	7.5	29.2	29.2	24.3	7.8	1.3
FOOD SCI.TECH SL	18	5.94					17.6	70.6	11.8
MARINE SCI. SL	357	4.09	0.3	11.8	25.5	24.6	21.8	10.6	5.3
NOS SL	157	4.38		11.5	12.8	25.0	30.8	16.0	3.8
PHYSICS HL	15,030	4.80	0.3	4.8	17.4	21.0	21.5	18.7	16.4
PHYSICS SL	12,888	4.21	0.7	10.6	26.1	23.0	18.1	12.6	9.0
SPORTS EX SCI HL	1,404	4.77	0.7	5.6	13.3	21.1	25.6	22.5	11.1
SPORTS EX SCI SL	4,492	3.92	0.9	13.2	27.0	26.5	20.1	9.2	3.2
ENV. AND SOC. SL Individuals and societies/Sciences	19,991	4.22	1.5	8.3	22.5	25.8	23.6	13.0	5.4

source: https://www.ibo.org/globalassets/new-structure/about-the-ib/pdfs/dp-cp-provisional-statistical-bulletin-may-2023.pdf

The big three here are Biology, Chemistry, and Physics. What can we infer?

Don't let the high percentage of 7's for Physics HL fool you. The students that take Physics HL are exactly the type of students you would expect to score 7s.

The mean grades for all three are relatively similar. I think with group 4 subjects it comes down to choosing something that you will enjoy and where the material is relatively easier.

If sciences aren't your strong suit, it is recommended that you pick environmental systems and societies, which is an interdisciplinary course that can either count as a social science or a science. This class is known to be on the easier side, and if offered at your school, is a great way to "get out of" doing science. I must add that this course is only offered at SL, so you will have to take a different course at HL (such as a language).

Otherwise, Biology HL (since you still need one more) is another good pick. Yes, it's a lot of memorization, but it is 'easier' than Physics or Chemistry – which are known to be notoriously rigorous.

Biology is basically pure memory work. There is much less 'thinking' than in the other subjects – and that is probably to your benefit.

Important note: if you are intending to pursue medicine then your choice will be very much different here. It's almost always required to take both chemistry and biology if you wish to study medicine at university level.

Similarly, if you want to study something engineering or physics related, you should choose physics. Don't make the mistake of choosing physics just because you have a small interest in it. Even at SL, the content is pretty hard.

Recommendation: Biology HL or ESS SL

GROUP 5

Now, onto mathematics. It has been 4 years since they revamped the math courses, so let's take a look at the M23 stats:

Subject	Candidates	Mean Grade	% 1	% 2	% 3	% 4	% 5	% 6	% 7
MATH ANALYSIS HL	20,719	4.87	0.9	5.5	11.2	21.4	24.7	21.6	14.7
MATH ANALYSIS SL	38,953	4.61	1.1	6.4	15.6	22.9	24.7	19.2	10.0
MATH APPS HL	6,985	4.37	2.0	10.6	15.5	24.3	23.5	15.7	8.3
MATH APPS SL	40,293	3.87	5.9	15.9	19.4	23.5	19.4	11.5	4.4

source: https://www.ibo.org/globalassets/new-structure/about-the-ib/pdfs/dp-cp-provisional-statistical-bulletin-may-2023.pdf

The math curriculum has two different types: Analysis and Approaches (AA) or Applications and Interpretations (AI). Generally, difficulty can be ranked as follows: AI SL, AA SL, AI HL, AA HL.

If you are studying physics, math, engineering, or a very math intensive major then you should definitely choose AA HL.

If you are studying business or econ universities might accept both or prefer HL AI. However, be alert: most business and economics programs **do not** accept AI SL.

If you aren't going to study something that needs a lot of mathematics I'd still suggest that you choose AA SL only because some universities will react poorly if they see that you chose the easiest course (AI SL). However, this is not always the case, so please do research into some potential programs and their admission programs. If you really struggle with math then there is no harm in taking AI SL.

The big difference between AI and AA lies in the fact that AA is much more algebra-based, while AI puts the emphasis on real-life applications. If you like math problems that just require one answer then do math AA, or if you are doing a math career or science job then definitely do AA. However, if you prefer longer word problems that are directly applicable to real life problems, then AI might be a better fit. In addition, the AI course includes a lot more statistics which can be very beneficial and applicable to social science careers.

Recommendation: Mathematics AA (SL)

GROUP 6

Finally, we are left with the Arts:

Subject	Candidates	Mean Grade	% 1	% 2	% 3	% 4	% 5	% 6	% 7
DANCE HL	361	4.83		2.5	12.5	23.5	32.3	19.0	10.2
DANCE SL	436	4.32		4.0	32.5	21.0	19.5	15.8	7.3
FILM HL	2,645	4.51	0.7	6.0	13.0	29.8	27.8	18.1	4.7
FILM SL	1,749	4.15	1.1	7.8	20.6	34.5	20.3	12.4	3.3
MUSIC HL	1,401	4.78	0.2	2.1	13.9	23.8	30.9	21.4	7.7
MUSIC SL	1,665	4.16	0.6	4.5	26.7	32.8	21.1	10.8	3.5
THEATRE HL	2,306	5.00	0.4	2.0	7.6	24.8	28.2	26.7	10.3
THEATRE SL	1,215	4.61	0.3	4.6	13.4	30.3	26.3	17.5	7.7
VISUAL ARTS HL	9,890	4.39	0.2	3.2	21.5	30.8	24.5	15.9	3.8
VISUAL ARTS SL	5,842	4.01	0.3	5.5	24.5	41.8	19.1	7.7	1.1

source: https://www.ibo.org/globalassets/new-structure/about-the-ib/pdfs/dp-cp-provisional-statistical-bulletin-may-2023.pdf

So, what can we infer from that table?

Not that many positives, to be honest. If faced with the choice of having another Group 3 (or 4) subject or a Group 6, I think you are much better off choosing a Group 3.

There will be those who wish to pursue one of these Group 6 topics at university level, and in that case then by all means go ahead and take that subject.

Pro Tip: make sure to check how these subjects are assessed. It's not that you get graded for how pretty your drawings are in Visual Art – there is a serious verbal examination.

I would only suggest choosing one of these if you are very passionate about it- it isn't even about talent.

Recommendation: in general, steer clear of all of these.

Interdisciplinary Subjects:

We still need to address the interdisciplinary subjects

Interdisciplinary Subjects Grade Distribution

Subject	Subject Groups	Candidates	Mean Grade	% 1	% 2	% 3	% 4	% 5	% 6	% 7
ENV. AND SOC. SL	Individuals and societies/Sciences	14,423	4.16	1.8	8.0	24.3	25.5	23.7	11.8	4.8
LIT AND PERF SL	Studies in Language and Literature/The Arts	530	4.56		2.0	16.7	30.2	29.8	16.9	4.4

source: https://www.ibo.org/contentassets/bc850970f4e54b87828f83c7976a4db6/dp-statistical-bulletin-may-2019-en.pdf

<u>REMINDER:</u> ESS is both a Group 4 AND Interdisciplinary subject (Group 5)

Environmental systems and societies is a course that looks like an attractive course as a standard level interdisciplinary course. It's pretty easy in its content, however my main problem with it is that it is only offered at SL.

Thus, if you had to choose between Bio HL and ESS SL, I still recommend Bio HL because it will fill up an HL for you.

Subject Group Data

Finally, below is a breakdown of grade distribution by subject group:

Group	Candidates	Mean Grade	% 1	% 2	% 3	% 4	% 5	% 6	% 7
Studies in Language and Literature	134,010	4.82	0.0	0.9	7.6	29.9	35.3	22.5	3.7
Language acquisition	101,457	5.24	0.1	1.7	7.1	17.4	27.2	32.4	14.1
Individuals and societies	159,102	4.74	0.4	4.3	11.5	25.0	29.9	21.6	7.2
Sciences	130,408	4.35	1.3	9.2	20.1	23.9	21.8	15.6	8.0
Mathematics	106,950	4.37	2.9	10.0	16.2	22.9	22.6	16.6	8.7
The arts	27,510	4.38	0.4	4.2	19.7	32.3	24.0	15.1	4.3
Interdisciplinary	20,315	4.23	1.4	8.2	22.4	25.7	23.8	13.1	5.4
Total	**679,752**	**4.67**	**0.9**	**5.2**	**13.1**	**24.6**	**27.5**	**21.0**	**7.8**

source: https://www.ibo.org/globalassets/new-structure/about-the-ib/pdfs/dp-cp-provisional-statistical-bulletin-may-2023.pdf

We can infer several things from this table.

First, notice the high percentage of students obtaining a grade 7 for Language acquisition. Remember what I told you about kids taking a language they are already very comfortable with as a B?

Yep, that's them right there. Accordingly, the mean grade for Language acquisition is considerably better than the rest of the groups.

Second, notice the low percentage of students scoring 7's in the arts – that's why I suggested steering clear of the entire group (**unless... this is your passion / future career path!**)

What if our recommendation is not available at your school?

Well, that's just life. No need to get angry or upset about things that are outside of your control.

As aforementioned, you can look into self-taught study, however my advice would just be to pick the best combination of subjects out of what is available to you.

Getting a second opinion (and a third)

Ok so let's say you think you have picked the best 6 subjects for you, what now?

I highly suggest you hop your ass online and go and ask IB kids and alumni if you have made the correct choice and what you should expect

Forums are great places to ask such questions. To make answering easier, please be sure to include your choices and if they are SL or HL as well as your:

- Interests
- Plan for after IB (university course)
- Competence level (e.g. are you good at math?)

This will lead to much better tailored responses.

> **Pro Tip:** use the Reddit r/IBO forum or discord to ask 80,000+ kids if your subject choices are the best ones for you.

Changing Subjects

So, let's say you chose your 6 subjects but a few months into your IB journey, you think you have made a terrible mistake. What now?

If you really think you've cocked up, I suggest talking to your IB coordinator, as well as the involved subject teachers, **as soon as possible.** If it's something like dropping to SL, that shouldn't be too much hassle and can even be done halfway throughout your IB (as long as you have an HL to back it up with).

If you want to change an entire subject then you should make this decision no later than a month into your study, and even then you should be extra polite and courteous to your school faculty as they can be very anal about these things (understandably sometimes, as administrative things can be a headache).

CHAPTER 5

HOW TO SUCCEED IN THE IB CLASSROOM

*'If you think you're doing the IB, you're wrong.
The IB is doing you.'*

The purpose of this chapter is to provide some basic guidelines and daily advice that you should follow to survive in the world of IB. The degree to which you follow the advice in this chapter depends on what type of student you are.

If organization, motivation and promptness are second nature to you then you will find most of the information in this chapter somewhat obvious.

Attendance

Although some of your classmates may beg to differ, missing school does not make you a modern-day Ferris Bueller. You must ensure that you are attending class as often as you can. Most of your classes are very demanding, and even one or two days missed could mean a lot of hassle in terms of catching up with the material.

No matter how useless you think a certain class is, I would still recommend you show up because it is good work ethic and it will keep you busy.

In the rare case that you miss class because of an illness or any other valid reason, make sure that you talk to your teacher and get the correct material that you may have missed.

Those of you who skip class regularly will find that sympathy is hard to come by when you have a genuine reason for your tardiness. This is yet another reason to avoid unnecessarily skipping class.

Free Periods

The term 'free period' has varying interpretations from student to student and school to school. To some of you this may mean an hour of playing solitaire on your laptop, to others it may mean an opportunity to finish last night's homework. Similarly, some schools are more stringent than others. At my school, most teachers treated 'free periods' as a quiet one-hour study session where students were free to do work independently. I want you to make the most of the time available. Whether you do work, socialize, or catch up on sleep – make sure that it is not time wasted and that you are doing something that will benefit your grades in the long run.

> **Pro Tip:** don't sleep in your free period – it will be uncomfortable and might mess up your sleep cycle. Save it for a power nap at home!

Some schools allow students to arrive later (if the free periods are in the morning) or to depart before school is over (if the free periods are in the afternoon). Find out if you can do the same and decide whether you would benefit from this. On occasion, I would try to miss any free period at the end of the day and get home to catch up on some sleep. You need to work out whether this is possible, and feasible.

Understandably, some schools simply do not allow students to have 'free periods'. Many of you studying in the US will find that any period not devoted to the IB will be packed with an alternative high school curriculum. Some schools prefer to devote more time to extra-curricular activities or keep students busy with extra classes. If this is the case, then great. If you are being kept busy and productive, then you are on the right track.

Note Taking

Personally, I was never that great at taking notes in class. My handwriting was poor, and I found it difficult to take in everything that was being discussed and simultaneously jot down effective notes. I figured that if I can engage in the conversation and understand what the teacher is trying to say, then I could write down more effective notes after class. Unfortunately, too often I would forget.

Effective note taking is not something that can be mastered in a few months, let alone a few weeks. It took me nearly two years of university lectures to finally be able to write and process information fast enough to take very helpful notes.

I find that this habit differs in difficulty across students. If handwriting is your biggest concern, try to bring a laptop. A more drastic alternative (and one that should only be used during the most important and difficult sessions) would be to bring a voice recorder and make notes afterwards.

Of course, this involves a great deal of dedication and motivation, however I do remember certain HL Mathematics classes where a voice recorder proved to be a lifesaver.

> **Pro Tip:** if you can use laptops in class, organize a group of students to use a Google doc and take notes together in a collective file!

There are two key things to remember when taking notes. One is to make sure that everything you write down isn't already explained in detail in your textbook and/or previous notes. This is very inefficient, and you are better off simply listening and letting the information seep into your memory. The second thing to keep in mind is to only write down notes that make sense. If you find yourself writing words that are unfamiliar to you, then you are wasting your time. You need to raise your hand and ask the question.

You may find yourself lucky enough to have a friend or two who takes outstanding notes. Although getting great notes from a fellow peer is better than having nothing at all, I would still be cautious before resorting to this option. No matter how good the notes are, they will never be as valuable to you as something you wrote down yourself.

In recent years with the rising popularity of Instagram, some students have begun to take great pride in their notes and photograph their handwritten works of art. They are called 'studyspo' or 'studygrams'– and it is worth checking them out. It may inspire you to perhaps start taking clearer and better notes. Whether this will help you memorize the material better is an altogether different question.

A possible way of note organizing my friend taught me in the beginning of DP, and it was perfect for me. You have one A4 notebook with holes for every subject, where you put your notes in. At the end of the week, you go through it, carefully rip those that are of value (not just random calculations etc.) and put in a separate subject-dedicated folder. However, if you may need them next week, you keep them in too. The same goes for all printed material your teacher gives you. This way your backpack is lighter and you have a pretty folder to revise before summatives through.

Organization

If only I had an IB point for every time I heard someone mutter the words 'what, we had homework?' Keeping an agenda or a daily planner is a very simple solution to keeping track of what is due when. Make a habit of writing down important dates as soon as you hear about them. The IB does a pretty good job at reminding students about the big deadlines (Extended Essay, External Assessments, CAS portfolio). However, any internal deadlines you may have are your responsibility to note.

There's no reason to go old-school when it comes to organization. With the rise in popularity of iPhones, and personal laptops, it has become much easier for you to electronically set reminders. These items are also more likely to be consulted, and less likely to be lost than a simple paperback agenda.

One of the greatest tools you've probably seen on the internet is Notion. I've created a page that incorporated everything school-related: a big to-do list, reminders of important tasks to be done, a calendar and a week planner with a to-do list for each day.

Bonus 1: *Monday morning or Sunday evening write everything you have planned for the week, and then assign it 1-3 days in advance. Something I did was put the most work on Monday, pressuring myself at the beginning of the week. Worst-case scenario you will still have time on the weekend, best-case scenario you will have more time for quality rest after these rough days.*

Bonus 2: *one of the ways to organize your page is to create a gallery with every subject + CAS, EE, TOK, and all college admissions related things. In each page you create a to-do list for this subject, an IA page for checklists, methodologies, primary research etc., and just throw in everything you may find useful. This is a quick way to see visually where you're falling behind in your studies as you see the checklists.*

Homework

When it comes to homework, it is very difficult to prescribe specific advice because people have different preferences that work best for them. Personally, I found that doing homework in the late evening or at night was the most effective. This worked for me as there were little distractions and there was a sense of urgency which kept me motivated.

Besides timing, you also need to consider working effectively for concentrated amounts of times with no breaks. Ideally, working for 20 minutes non-stop with no outside interference and then rewarding yourself with a small break seems to be among the ideal strategies. Some of you may find that you work best with music in the background, or that your multitasking skills are so good that you can afford to flip your computer tabs from Facebook to iTunes to your lab report every few minutes. It's difficult to change this habit, and unless it is seriously damaging to the quality of your work, I would not worry too much about it.

One tip that I found to work very nicely when doing homework was to save my favorite material for last. Getting all the difficult and less-favorable work out of the way early will not only lessen the chances of simply not doing it, but you will also have something to look forward to.

Of course, one should be careful not to rush through the harder material just for the sake of 'getting it out the way' before moving onto the more enjoyable material.

Be heard

No matter how timid and shy you may be, there will be days when you simply need to make a formal comment or complaint about something that concerns you. In order to do this, you need to build a constructive relationship with your IB Coordinator and any other influential teachers. This is much easier said than done.

> **Pro Tip:** sit in front of the class – every day, all day. Yes, you might look like a keen loser, but honestly sitting in the front of the class was a huge revelation for me. It kept me focused and lessened distractions.

Learn how to talk to authoritative figures. If you book a meeting with your IB Coordinator, then do not show up unprepared. If you show them that you care, they will care too. The same goes for most teachers. If you show an interest and a longing for help (perhaps by asking for a contact email or number to reach them at after-school hours) then they are more than likely to respond positively.

Procrastination

So, you now know how to maximize productivity and you're thinking that planning and getting on top of all your work seems like a pretty swell idea, but you have one major problem left: procrastination. It is one thing to plan and be organized, but it is another thing to follow that plan and get things done because they aren't going to get done by themselves.

Here are 5 easy steps to beat procrastination:

1. Just 5 minutes – start the task just for 5 minutes. Just do 5 minutes. Chances are, you'll be able to start, if not try any of the following.

2. Break it down – putting on your planner "Do EE" is a large and unreasonable task. Break it down into smaller chunks and work with one chunk at a time; e.g. gather research for EE. And then just do that (and tick it off). Each day do a little more until it gets going. If the task is too hard for you, see what you can do first, then seek help after.

3. Get away from your laptop/phone/internet – put it in a different room or turn it off. Honestly, I know how distracting Instagram or Tiktok is when you are in the mood to procrastinate. You'll find you will get going as soon as you can't get to it. If you need your laptop, use an app like Self Control to block your "procrastination sites".

4. Plan a reward – "After I do this, I can do whatever I want for the rest of the evening." Or, promise yourself that if you do everything you

planned to during the week, you can take the weekend off – now that's a good deal!

5.   Keep busy – don't leave yourself a ridiculous amount of time to do minuscule homework tasks that you'll put off anyway. Get involved! Go and play sports, hang out with friends, volunteer, then see how well you work afterwards. Don't give yourself the time to procrastinate.

Procrastination is horrible. I hate it loads and I have a half decent way of sorting it out. Just know that you cannot get rid of it completely otherwise you'll probably end up not enjoying life. No one can seize every single opportunity they must work. It's just not realistic.

One of the reasons why procrastination happens is because there are two parts of your brain. One part sees the short-term benefit of everything, like going on Tiktok or staring into the sky. This part is much bigger than the part that sees the long-term benefit of working now. Plus, the long-term benefit part (the determined one) gets tired quickly. Ok, now imagine yourself as two people: 'present' you, and 'future' you.

What you need to remember is that it isn't now that you will be feeling the consequences of your procrastination, it will be 'future' you. You need to look to future you and think that you want to have less work, so you'll do it now.

Procrastination isn't because you're lazy; it's because you're weak in the sight of distractions (that sounds mean, but everyone gets distracted for the reason I stated above). Some overall advice:

- Keep your work neat. You don't want to be revising and realize that you cannot read half of anything that you've written. Some care will go a long way.

- You don't need to write full sentences when making notes, just something that can remind you what was taking place in class.

- Try organizing your work daily. This further reduces the chances of losing sheets and notes, hole punch it and keep it safe. You'd be surprised how much they can help.

- Lessen the distractions!

- Delete some social media apps or set yourself time limits. You'll be shocked how many hours you can spend on Tiktok, Instagram or Netflix.

- Mute your computer so you aren't hearing all sorts of notifications. Same goes for putting your phone off. Not on silent or vibrate – OFF.

- Clear the cookies from your computer so you must enter your password every time you want to log into something. This makes logging into stuff an added effort so you're more inclined to just not bother and start your work. This process is automated if you use 'incognito mode' on your browser.

- Give yourself motivation

- Put pictures up of what you want to achieve (e.g. a 45-point diploma?)

- Plan a little treat you can have only if you've completed a certain amount of work, not if you've done something for a specific time. It's too easy to say, 'I've read for half an hour, time to chill'.

Also, there is such a thing as 'helpful' procrastination. So, when you feel lazy instead of refreshing the Instagram homepage, read an article from the news or a page from a book relating to your subjects. Or read a few more chapters from this book! In addition, don't mistake procrastination for having a break, breaks are good. They keep your sanity intact.

There is a fundamental cognitive difference between procrastinators and normal people. Everyone gets overwhelmed by work sometimes. Even the busiest or most efficient people might feel overwhelmed when there's too much work and not enough time. But the procrastinator is different. The procrastinator might have plenty of time, however he puts off work until there isn't enough time and then feels scared, stressed and overwhelmed. This means the procrastinator makes his own life much worse – does that sound like anyone you know?

This sort of behavior has a massive effect on our IB scores, both in exams and especially because of coursework. By putting things off and avoiding work we leave ourselves no time to work well. There's no time to complete tasks to our satisfaction and we end up with worse scores and worse universities than we could have reached.

So why do we keep procrastinating? When we keep making poor decisions which are illogical, the reason is almost always an emotional one. The three most common causes of chronic procrastination are fear, anxiety and shame. This could be fear that the work won't be good enough, that it won't score high enough, that peers will be better etc. Whatever the reason, it is emotional and causes real problems. Fortunately, the problem tells us the solution.

Let's say you have a big project to do – maybe your Extended Essay, maybe revision for the IB exams. Whatever it is, you might find yourself procrastinating. If you're honest with yourself this is probably because you're worried that it won't be good enough. This is because the procrastinator only sees giant goals – so he sees 'The IB' as one goal, or Extended Essay as a goal. Of course, these are impossibly big goals to act upon. But the non-procrastinator sees things differently. Non-procrastinators realize big goals are just groups of small tasks. While doing the EE might seem impossible, googling the markscheme, emailing your teacher for guidance and looking at the textbook are all easy tasks. And this is the secret: seemingly impossible tasks are just made of lots of very possible smaller tasks!

To change from a procrastination mindset to a non-procrastination one is not really that hard. The next time you start to feel nervous about a task grab a piece of paper and start to list all the things necessary to complete that task.

Maybe to do an essay you would have to: do background research, find appropriate books, make a mind map, make a plan, write, edit and submit. Now focus on the first thing: for example, the research. What small tasks does the first thing include? Google the question, look at Wikipedia articles, look at the textbook. Now do that first small task, like checking the Wikipedia article on a certain topic.

That's it! You're working! Keep doing that over and over again and the essay will finish itself. It is possible to rewire your procrastinator brain. Now that you know how, test it out. Even at this moment you have things to do...yep! You just thought of one right? Probably one you really don't want to do. So, grab some paper right now, I'll wait... Good! Now write the task name at the top and just start listing all things you have to do in that task. Ok, now write all the subtasks. If it looks too hard, just keep doing this. When you think you can do the first task, get going! And good luck!

Time Management

The best advice I can give is <u>time management</u> and <u>organization</u>. I genuinely don't think you can succeed in IB if you don't know how to properly manage and organize your time. I also think the timeline of when you finish internal assessments is a major deciding factor in how efficiently you can study for exams. So, here are a few pointers:

Dividing your time equally between your subjects:

My time was mainly divided between 3-4 subjects. English, I did not allocate during the week unless I was working on a written task or something. Dutch I worked on whenever we had homework, maybe for 2-3 times a week, I would spend around one hour. The ideal is to spend 2 hours for each of your SLs and 3-4 hours on your HLs weekly.

That would be 3 hours of studying daily (weekdays). Mind again that this is not a number of hours you strictly have to abide by, because quality over quantity. Sometimes you have to work for more than this during the busy IA period. I would use the weekends to study for exams if I had any, or revise my math and physics for the week, my two most challenging subjects.

Efficient use of time in Holidays:

Going into IB you really must mentally prepare yourself for the fact you're going to need to sacrifice your holidays for the most part, but then again this really depends on your target score. I have classmates who enjoyed all their holidays for the most part, and still managed to get a 30-35 score.

However, I also do know people that regret not working during the holidays because you can really get so much done in them, which does reduce the stress of having so much work piled up.

It also gives you so much more time to get your work done with higher quality, and lastly gives you more room for improvement. What I'm trying to say here is: I really do think you should invest a lot of time in your holidays to get work done.

> **Pro Tip:** One thing I ALWAYS did in all of my long holidays in the two years (winter, spring, summer breaks) was brush up on my content for my hardest subjects.

I can safely say that the reason why I got 7s in my IAs and an A for my TOK and EE was because I started those essays in the holidays. I had plenty of time to plan, write and erase, and improve. Working on the holidays is a big plus because most probably your peers will not be working, and your teacher will be focused on looking at your work only.

So, write your drafts during the holidays, and email them to your teachers. **DON'T** keep thinking that you're bothering your teacher, if they don't have the time they will tell you, so do your part by starting early and sending your work frequently.

As soon as your holiday starts, write down the things you need to get done, then divide them into tasks and assign them to each day of your holiday (this step is so important, if you do not plan you will get overwhelmed with the work and end up doing nothing or doing it badly). Also, I found that it gets very boring if you focus on one single task for a long period of time.

Working on something for a long time, you can hit a block, you're uninspired and you're stuck, and you feel like you don't know how to continue. Stop, take a break, work on something else for the day and then go back with a new mindset.

Now in no way shape or form am I saying do not take time off, just be reasonable. Take a whole day or two off in the week, and then for the rest of the days just do 2-3 hours of study, or however long you need to finish the tasks you assigned for that day. Just wake up early and get them done, then enjoy the rest of your day.

Ideal Timeline for finishing IAs and starting to study (May exams)

(It is extremely crucial that you give yourself enough time to study for the externals/may exams. It is not easy to solidify your knowledge of two years' worth of content for 6 subjects in the short period of time you had. So, here is ideally how it goes.

- You start working on your EE winter break of DP year 1, considering you already chose your subject and research question. Most IB students finish their first draft of the EE in the summer break DP year 1.

- I would recommend alongside your EE, you choose two other IAs to work on. Leave the sciences for DP year 2 to allow yourself time in the summer to research your experiment well.

- TOK essay: students start it as soon as the topics are released in November DP year 2. I started mine in the winter break, in December of DP year 2. Not ideal, but I managed to finish by the due date and had time to write my second drafts.

- In the winter break of DP year 2, I wrote a pretty solid first draft for my science IAs, math IA, and TOK essay.

The latest date you want to be working on anything written is January 30th (this is just what I see ideal of course if there any unforeseeable problems it's not your fault, not everything will go as planned so don't sweat as long as you started early and done your job). I know the deadline isn't until April and no you will not be penalized, but here are the consequences of working on your IAs until April:

1. Your teachers will not have enough time to properly evaluate it and give you feedback

2. You are borrowing the precious time in which you should've been studying for your final exams

3. You will be extremely stressed because all the IAs have the same deadline, so you're going to slack and not meet the standards.

The reason I recommend you start working on these IAs so early is that you're going to keep editing them for so long. Second, third, fourth drafts. If you write your IA for the first time in March or April DP year 2, how are you going to know what could've been improved?

With that being said, it's great to start studying for your externals in February. That gives you around 3 months, which is plenty of time.

For a more complete guide (including subject specific advice), please consult my other book: 50 Tips, Tricks, and Secrets for the Successful International Baccalaureate [IB] Student

CHAPTER 6

HOW TO WIN FRIENDS AND INFLUENCE TEACHERS

'There are no significant others, only significant figures'

This chapter is not only important for your time in the IB program – but it is an essential skill to acquire if you want to be successful in life and get ahead.

The skill I'm referring to here is, in the crudest sense, the skill of getting what you want from people in higher positions of power.

You've probably already engaged in this in one form or other as a child manipulating your parents to get what you want, but as you get older the players in that game change, and your tactics adjust accordingly.

Now that being said, I would like to take a moment to remind you that being a teacher is one of the hardest and most underappreciated jobs in the world. There is no glamor, and the pay isn't proportional to the amount of effort (most) teachers put in.

Of all the people you will encounter in your short stay on this planet, your teachers are one of the few characters who genuinely want the best for you and care about your future and your well-being – and for that they deserve respect and gratitude. If you treat them well, you will get treated well in return.

Get used to it: teachers are your new best friends. Despite what teachers say, they do have favorite students and these lucky kids get preferential treatment (I was one of them). These students get this treatment as there is a greater level of trust and dialogue between them and the teacher, which makes the teacher more lenient. What does "lenient" entail, well...

Teachers will be more lenient when it comes to deadlines and will accept your work late and still give feedback allowing you to submit better versions of your work at later dates (this can be useful as time allows you to spot your own mistakes).

The feedback teachers give you will be more detailed and comprehensive as they believe their advice won't go to waste; hence, they don't mind the extra effort.

When the time comes to grading both report cards and predicted grades the teachers will be optimistic. They believe that you are a good student and over time you will progress; hence if you are within grade boundaries you are likely to get marked up.

> **Pro Tip:** foster good relations with your teachers from the very start – and in some cases even before you start IB. The extra engaged students even email their teachers over the summer to ask if there is any reading / work they should do...

Even better and more daring is the fact that you can discuss your grade. For example, if you know that it is important for you to get a 7 in physics (and you are getting high level 6s), you can discuss it with your teacher and ask them for that grade, justifying why you will be able to reach it. A few methods of justification would be as follows:

Show them your planned revision, for example if you will be attending any summer courses or if you have bought anything that can help you improve at the subject. This proof should be tangible and significant.

If you start the year with 5s in test and are ending on 7s, your teacher might be tempted to give you a 6; however you can show him or her that you actually have shown progress and you "believe" you deserve a 7 (and that you are confident of maxing out the marks on your IA).

You can have detailed and private conversations on matters such as homework, IAs, exams, tests and things that you don't understand in your subject. Remember all the information you receive is useful if used properly.

Don't forget it, teachers are humans too, they have their faults and they are usually very fun people. Get to know them and you will understand how they think, and ultimately how they grade. But even more than that, you will have a great time in class learning and interacting with these interesting people. I can say as a matter of fact that I liked all my teachers both as academics and as people, we got along very well and even joked around.

IB Coordinator

Although your interactions with this faculty member may be limited, they hold the key to your IB diploma – you do not want to piss this person off. Everything from choosing subjects to submitting crucial coursework on time, they will oversee.

Understandably IB coordinators will vary in experience from school to school but do your best to get on good terms and make sure they know how serious you are about achieving your diploma.

Remember that it's in this person's best interest to make sure the entire class does well on their IB. It will reflect poorly on them if students fail to get their diploma. For that reason, if there is something you feel will increase the scores of the students, you should share your thoughts with the coordinator. For example, if you feel like you need new textbooks or you feel like you desperately need to change class, they are the person to go and see.

In the following section I will go over a few key faculty members and try to explain the importance of fostering a healthy relationship. I am aware that not every school will be lucky enough to have a designated person for each role, but nonetheless the advice will be applicable.

> **Pro Tip:** if your IB coordinator is not very experienced – help them out! Lend them this book, teach them about IB coordinator resources (they have their own secret support groups on Facebook). Of course, avoid being belittling or depreciative of their work..

The Principal

The idea here is pretty simple – don't mess up and get into disciplinary trouble. Although they don't have an impact on your IB grades directly, they do have the power to kick you out of school if you are a jackass, so just don't be one.

Subject-Specific Teachers

Obviously, these faculty members are very important. From your IA work, to your predicted grades, to helping you revise for the subject – your daily teachers are instrumental to your IB success.

You will see them almost every day, so you better make a great first impression. If you show them that you care about getting top marks, they will provide you with the necessary tools.

Will you click and get along with each one of them? No, probably not. Some will be more problematic than others but learning the skill of getting past that is something that you will cherish for the rest of your life. You need to understand that part of the game here is just playing the part.

Do what they want you to do and then it will be much easier to ask them to do you favors.

Make sure to pay close attention to the details of the assignments that your teacher gives (yes, the details). Basically, you need to know exactly what your teachers want. It might even be worth asking alumni who have had your teacher in the past what they want and what they like.

Asking questions is also crucial to gaining your teacher's respect – basically don't be invisible, and don't let shyness get in the way of your learning.

If the teacher wants you to have a laptop and TI-84, have a laptop and TI-84. If they say you need a silver Mickey-Mouse balloon, have that. Don't skimp on required class supplies, even if inconvenient or expensive. It will handicap you. Again, you want to do everything you can to satisfy the teacher's expectations.

> **Pro Tip:** talk to IB alumni from your school to find out the best way to approach certain teachers and also what you can expect from being in their class. A good relationship with graduates is a very useful resource to have.

As covered in the chapter on subject choices – there will inevitably be teachers who you deem 'not good enough' to be teaching their subject. This happens, it's part of life. But that doesn't mean you have an excuse to just give up. You will need to take that subject much more seriously and do lots of independent study (this is great preparation for university). This is where our advice on revision and internal assessments will come in handy.

Keep in mind that the internal assessment means just that – *internal*. This means your teacher will be the one to give it a grade. Ultimately, a sample will be sent off to the IBO to be 'moderated' if marks are too high or too low, but this won't matter much if you've created such friction with your teacher that your IA marks are horrible. Teacher bias during IA marking is something that does occur, but you should be doing your best to mitigate this.

If there are some serious issues that can't be resolved with a certain teacher, you should seek to find a solution by approaching your IB coordinator. The hierarchy for resolving problems should be as such: teacher, then head of department (if there is one), then IB coordinator, then principal, then parents. Most problems can be overcome with simple dialogue.

Finally, be polite to your teachers / professors and subtly let them know you wish to succeed in their class. Don't be a suck up, but don't be rude or lazy either. Grading practices are never completely objective, despite what you might hear = or how hard teachers might try to make it so.

University Counsellor

Another extremely important individual – both for US and UK bound students. Plan a trip to their office sometime early in the first year – maybe even over the summer. Discuss your options and get as many resources as possible (they might have some great university application books in their office). The university counselor should help you with all things related to college applications, but you would also be wise to do some research on your own (and check out my other book on IB university application).

Grade Predictions

Your subject teachers (and EE/TOK for that matter) will be required to submit grade predictions for your university applications. Here is where student-teacher relationships are paramount.

> **Pro Tip:** find out what your school's policy is regarding grade predictions early on. When are they issued? Are they made available? Can they be changed?

Predicted grades are a tricky obstacle for any IB student. Nine times out of ten, students will feel that they are being under-predicted. Many schools refuse to disclose the predictions to students because they anticipate a large angry group of kids mobbing them with protests after school hours. Nonetheless, predicted grades are the golden ticket when it comes to university offers. If your predicted grades are below the usual entry standards, the chances of you receiving an offer from a UK university are slim to none.

Here is my simple advice when it comes to maximizing your chances of getting the best predicted grades: negotiation. The matter of the fact is that teachers often look at things like homework grades, test results and class participation as an indicator of how well you will do in the final IB examinations.

Although some of those things may play a small role, the truth is that the best predictors of your final results are: internal assessments (coursework that counts towards your final grade), how well you take IB examinations, how well you prepared in the few months before examinations, and a small element of random luck. Luck and exam revision aside, the other two components are fairly easy to analyze.

If your teachers insist on looking at test scores and random homework assignments as a way to judge your future success in the final exams, you need to persuade them that your high-scoring IA (which accounts for 20-50% of final subject grades in most subjects) and your ability to study past-paper questions and handle mock exams are both a far better indicator of how well you will do.

I understand that this is easier said than done, but I do remember spending a good week or so visiting various teachers after-hours to convince them that despite my so-so homework grades or sometimes uninspired class participation, I will score highly on my diploma because I know what counts and I know how to play the IB system. Those of you who have been reading this book carefully will know exactly what I am talking about.

Letter of Recommendation

It is imperative that the person who you choose to write your reference for university applications is not only highly literate, but more importantly can fill the reference full of praise and admiration.

Obviously, the person writing your reference should be closely related to the subject you intend to study at university. There are minor exceptions to this. For example, when I was applying to study economics, my economics teacher at school did not necessarily dislike me, however I did feel that they would not put all their efforts into writing a stand-out reference and perhaps it would not be as elegantly written.

Instead, I sought the help of my geography teacher (who happened to hold a PhD from LSE and had previously taught economics and business at a high school level). The teacher in question clearly saw a lot of potential in me, so I asked for help and got a wonderfully written reference in return. Whomever you seek for this task, make sure they are not going to write a generic reference but instead something personal and something that will make you stand out.

The real objective of student-teacher relations in the IB is: 'why do work when you can get others to do it for you?'; some people call it 'leverage'. Unfortunately, getting your teachers to help doesn't mean you can just laze at home and do nothing. You need to make life easy for them - make plans, make time to see them, organize everything, be ready when they ask you questions. If you keep up a disciplined image, they will be lots more likely to take you seriously.

Yes, I understand that some teachers are quite unfriendly or unknowledgeable and so you don't want to see them. That's alright too. Just make sure you have everything under control, and you haven't upset the wrong people.

Online Teachers

If you are stuck at a school with really subpar and inexperienced IB teaches, there may be another solution to your worries. You may try to consult the advice of experienced IB teachers that are not at your school...

This is a very delicate strategy and requires a lot of precision in how you approach it, so be warned that it is not for everyone.

There are a lot of IB teachers who upload lots of resources to their personal websites and are quite well-known in the IB world. You could attempt to email or contact them and try to get some help.

Now, the most important thing to digest here is that you are NOT trying to take advantage of these people. Do not email them with the subject heading 'look over my IA' or ask them something like that. I get these emails every week and they go straight into my deleted folder.

Only if I feel that the person is genuine and shows evidence that they have tried to solve the problem themselves, do I consider really helping them out. They need to demonstrate genuine effort, and a certain degree of courtesy when asking for assistance.

> **Pro Tip:** NEVER, under any circumstances, should you send your files to someone else on the internet who you do not personally know. This includes your IA and your EE. You never know where these files will end up. Be careful and use common sense!

Use your common sense when approaching these teachers. They are busy, they have their own classrooms. But if you write a well-worded heartfelt email with a specific problem, then there is a small chance they might reply.

Keep in mind there are now 100,000 IB Diploma kids taking exams every year, so the chances of getting a reply is less and less. However, if you are really stuck and can't find help anywhere else, then this might be an avenue to look into.

Be kind. Be considerate. Be genuine and honest.

IB Friendships

Friends are here to help you get through the IB and vice versa; it is therefore crucial that you surround yourself with the correct people. Throughout my 2 years of IB if it were not for certain friends, I would not have been able to get the grades that I got.

They reviewed my work, corrected mistakes they saw, helped me learn and explained things that I didn't understand. But most importantly, as cheesy as this may sound, your good friends will always be there for you.

I remember after the mock exams when a good friend of mine got a whopping 28% on his HL Math Paper 1. He was feeling horrible. I mean he had always been a great student: 7s in math during the MYP were no problem.

> **Pro Tip:** surround yourself with people smarter than you

But as you may know, HL Math is a totally different kind of beast. So, being one of his best friends, I really had to comfort him and help him recover. No, we didn't passionately cuddle or feed each other chocolate ice-cream, but instead I gave him my honest opinion about his results and how he wasn't working hard enough. I told him that he was going out too much, and that doing well in HL Math wasn't possible with minimal studying. Fast forward six months, and he came out with a solid 6 at the end of the IB Exams.

The beauty of having good friends is invaluable. They make you smile, laugh, and love. The quote that goes 'Friendship is like peeing on yourself: everyone can see it, but only you get the warm feeling that it brings!' (Robert Bloch) is so true.

Don't seek quantity. One really good friend is better than three or four average ones. Spend time with people that you connect with, want to learn from, and genuinely enjoy conversing with. No, don't do it for the popularity aspect or seek people to validate your ego. You are better than that and you know it.

Your Squad

You will almost certainly develop a core group of friends within your IB classes. Try to be friends with students who have similar goals and aspirations as you, stay away from the troublemakers and keep in mind that it's not 'cool' to be a total failing slacker. It's good to have a group with different genders, cultures, and nationalities. Being at an IB school means you are likely exposed to a myriad of cultures – make the most of this so you can enrich yourself with other perspectives.

> **Pro Tip:** if you have high ambitions and want to really succeed in this program, then seek out like-minded individuals. You will really grow better as a team.

With your closest group of IB friends, I suggest you guys keep a WhatsApp group or a snapchat group open together. Surprisingly, this makes it easier to motivate and help each other. There are no better comforting words to an IB student than 'I haven't started it either'. Studying with your close IB squad over digital mediums is also an invaluable practice if done correctly.

Competition

The most important thing I can say about your in-class friendships is this: remember that the IB is not a competition amongst you. As in, marks are not standardized, certainly not in your classes. If you all deserve a grade 7, all of you will get a grade 7. Just because you get a very good mark on an assignment, does not mean that others cannot also get good marks. This means that there is a great incentive to help each other out and not withhold anything from each other.

I'm not saying copy and share your work; I am merely suggesting that you get the idea of 'competition amongst my peers' out of your head because there is no such thing. You should see your entire IB friend-group as one team, and you want everyone on that team to do well because you are not competing against each other.

So effectively that means you should study together. You should lend them your spare calculator if they forgot theirs. You should double-check the spelling and grammar in their IA if they ask you kindly. Within limits, you should have a very productive and co-operative friendship with your close IB friends.

Never Ask Them How Much Work They Did

This is a mistake that everyone makes, constantly. I even kept making it through my university experience. The dreaded questions: 'How much have you studied? How much work have you done?'

They are dreadful because the answer will never be something that you want to hear, nor helpful to you in any way.

If they say they have studied less than you – you might get a false sense of comfort. You might (foolishly) think to yourself that you are ahead of schedule and that you are on top of your work.

If they say they have studied less than you – you might get into a panic. You might freak out that you can never 'catch up' to how many hours they have done.

Keep in mind that people lie all the time about this stuff (I have no idea why). Also, one person's efficiency in revision might be completely different to another's.

I have known some absolute geniuses that only needed to work for an hour or two a day, but they were super productive. At the same time, some people are susceptible to distractions so 'five hours' of revision for them is actually equal to an hour of revision for the efficient person.

Pro Tip: avoid asking these questions and getting into these discussions. It helps nobody. Instead get together with your friends and study together

Most importantly: just try to be a good human being and the rest will follow. Treat others like you want to be treated and don't be an asshole to anyone.

CHAPTER 7

HOW TO USE THE INTERNET

'You know, the internet is not just for IB memes and cat videos'

This may be the most important chapter in the entire book.

Learning how to properly search for files, information, and advice from other IB students is an incredibly important skill that takes some time to truly master. In this chapter, I will break down basically everything you need to know about IB help on the internet and which resources you must consult in order to maximize your chances of success.

My advice is to read this chapter carefully in its entirety and test out every resource listed here – so you know for sure how to use it.

How to Google Sh*t ?

Okay, so this one may seem pretty obvious. If you have a question or are looking for a specific resource – Google should be your first point of consultation.

You should know all the basic tricks like using quotations when you want to search for a specific phrase, and knowing how to filter your search results to date ranges etc.

Specific Question

If there is a specific question you want to search for (in the hopes of finding the answer) then just type a section of the question in quotations and Google will try to locate the source. If you want to find the past paper / mark scheme that it came from, you can try to add 'pdf' after your quotations.

Specific Papers

Same advice as above, however better tips for finding papers are found below under the resources section.

Specific Books

If you want to find the answer booklet for a book you are using in class, you can also use the above advice. If searching for a full textbook, I suggest using lib-gen (explained below).

News Articles

This advice is pretty specific to those taking Economics (and Geography) but if you need a news article for a commentary then this is the way to do it (also works for TOK articles):

1. Go to Google

2. Search for a keyword like "tariffs" or whatever you wish to write about

3. Select NEWS in the search tabs

4. Click on Tools

5. Select a date range (e.g. 6 months)

6. Pick a recent article about from a reputable source

Explanations on Concepts

The internet is full of great resources that can give you extra insight on topics. Simply add 'IB' to the end of your search to get the most relevant videos or study notes. One great (free) resource is BlitzNotes, for classes like chemistry, economics and more.

Reddit

Okay, this is a big one. I probably spend about 2 to 3 hours on Reddit every damn day. I spend more time on Reddit than I do on social media or watching TV or playing video games. It's where I get my news from, it's where I come for entertainment, and it's where thousands of IB kids come to discuss things

What is Reddit?

Reddit is a social news aggregation, web content rating, and discussion website. Registered members submit content to the site such as links, text posts, and images, which are then voted up or down by other members. Posts are organized by subject into user-created boards called "subreddits", which cover a variety of topics including news, science, movies, video games, music, books, fitness, food, and image-sharing. Submissions with more up votes appear towards the top of their subreddit.

How do I use Reddit?

Go to www.reddit.com and create an account, then subscribe to any 'subreddits' that you are interested in. For IB specific content:

r/IBO

At www.reddit.com/r/ibo you will find the primary IB subreddit. By their description:

"This is the unofficial subreddit for all things concerning the International Baccalaureate. This subreddit encourages questions, constructive feedback, and the sharing of knowledge and resources among IB students, alumni, and teachers. Note that the subreddit is not run by the International Baccalaureate."

At the time of writing, it has over **150,000 registered subscribers.**

Pros: honestly, r/IBO is a lifesaver. It is an excellent community, and the moderators are top-notch. They constantly post the newest links to the best resources, and everybody is super-friendly. Every day roughly 15-30 different questions are posted and answered. If you post a question in the morning, you will almost always get a competent answer before lunch.

Cons: in recent years it has become a little bit 'meme-heavy'. For example, if you want to see the top posts for the last month and you sort by top, 90% of them will be upvoted memes. This isn't really a problem if you take some time to learn how to filter out memes and make the most of their weekly discussion threads.

Another problem is that people who are not comfortable with Reddit as a platform will unlikely to adopt r/IBO. It's usually already established redditors who are the most active, which is a shame as I'm sure non-redditors have lots of potential positive contributions.

If at first you find Reddit as a whole a little strange and the interface annoying – don't worry. That's often the first impression. It takes time to get used to.

The best way to understand why r/IBO is so great is to go there and check it out for yourself.

Make sure to check out Reddit-browsing apps for your mobile devices.

> **Pro Tip:** I would strongly encourage you to get to grips with how Reddit works as soon as possible. Some of the most successful IB students are Redditors (The average score of people who chose to answer their M19 survey was 35.75, 6 points above the IB global average of 29.63.)

r/IBresources

Another subreddit on Reddit that only came into existence in the last few years. In their own words:

'This subreddit aims to improve accessibility to available resources for IB students! To help them prepare and assimilate the knowledge and

information that fellow IB students need and require for their course in IB'

Basically, it's almost exclusively a forum for resources – thus it is a lot less active than r/IBO. At the time of writing, it has **6.7k** subscribers.

IBdocuments.com

This is the r/IBO affiliated host website for ALL the past papers and resources that you need. As aforementioned, these websites get taken down faster than you can say 'markscheme', so there is a good chance that the website may not be up anymore when you are reading this.

UPDATE 25/07/2024 – at the time of writing, the *original* website www.ibdocuments.com is *down*. However, a quick google search for 'ibdocument.com' will yield several mirror websites.

There are books, past papers, questionbanks – everything really. All easy to access and free.

If the website is down, check ibdocuments.com ibresources.github.io or ib.redditor.website.

If that doesn't work, your best bet is to go on r/IBO and just ask – someone will answer with a working link or email you what you need.

They have written a very handy guide on how to *use* the resources and what they entail:

https://www.ibdocuments.com/github/IBGUIDE.html

> **Pro Tip:** once you are on an IB resources website with documents that you need – **DOWNLOAD EVERYTHING** that is applicable to your subjects and store it offline because that website will go down when you need it most.

Facebook

It is my understanding that Facebook is falling out of favor with many kids choosing Instagram as their primary social media outlet, however there is one group on Facebook which I think is very important and one where I am an admin:

IB Students Worldwide

(www.facebook.com/groups/IBStudents)

This is a very active Group with over **16k** members currently. By their own description:

'A student-run group for International Baccalaureate Diploma Programme (IBDP) students. Formed in Sep 2017.'

Pros: a very well-run group with rules that are enforced and a good policy of accepting members who are actual diploma students. If you ask a question here, you can expect a good answer within an hour.

Cons: you need to have Facebook. Also, there is no 'sort by' option – so it's a bit random which posts get seen the most. There are significantly less memes than on r/IBO but that could change as time goes on.

Discord

Discord is a VoIP application designed initially for the video gaming community—that specializes in text, image, video and audio communication between users in a chat channel. Imagine Skype – but with hundreds of IB kids chatting at once.

The IB discord invite link is: https://discordapp.com/invite/ibo

It has over **10k members** and at any given time there are roughly 1000 users online.

Discord can be a bit confusing to use which is why you should read through the rules once you join. There will be people online who will help you out if you get confused.

Pros: as it is basically a large IB chatroom, you get instant responses. There are different 'rooms' for different subjects, and it is pretty well organized and moderated.

Cons: it's especially popular amongst gamers, so you might need to get used to that community aspect of it. Those who haven't used it before are usually put off by the interface. It can become a distraction if you don't use it wisely.

YouTube

We are lucky to have so many IB educators post free videos on the YouTube platform. There are a number of outstanding IB channels that truly made a difference in my IB journey. Don't dismiss YouTube as a valuable learning tool – particularly if you are a visual learner.

YouTube has amazing IB teachers. A lot of them are better than your IB teachers at school. A lot of them will also do past paper drills and go over questions. For an updated list of YouTube channels:

https://www.reddit.com/r/IBO/comments/75qbdw/ultimate_list_of_ib_youtube_teachers_and_other/

Again, this list is not definitive. I strongly recommend searching the forums I mentioned above for the most up to date compilation of YouTube resources. In addition, don't be scared to use some AP or A-level tutorials and videos. Often these three programs intersect, and if you know your syllabus for this topic, which the syllabus guide exists for, the explanation will in the end be roughly the same.

Quester.io

Quester is a relatively new platform, but it is the ultimate platform to find any and all resources you might need. When first clicking on the site, you might be overwhelmed by the vast amount of clickable links. To start, navigate to the IB resources page (using the left-hand drop-down menu), and start to explore all the resources that are available. This site has links to good YouTube tutors (such as the organic chemistry tutor), links to notes (I highly recommend the revisions sheets and syllabus summaries), and an endless amount of practice questions and even (sometimes) past papers. The site is chaotic and a bit unorganized, so do take some time to discover which resources will prove to be beneficial to you!

To save you some time, I will list my favorite resources which I have found for the subjects I took. This is not an exhaustive list, but a great start:

- Practice questions:
    - https://pestle-ib.firebaseapp.com/login (free)
    - https://paperplainz.com/ (paid)
    - https://www.revisionvillage.com/ (paid)
- Youtube: MSJ Chem, the organic chemistry tutor, Andy Masley, Chris Doner, OSC, EconplusDal

Kognity

Kognity is an online textbook resource that has saved my grade countless times. It is an interactive textbook, which contains practice questions for each subtopic. Although I would say that these questions don't accurately reflect the difficulty of the IB exams, they are a great way to start off your revision. In addition, this textbook contains great explanations that are often straight to the point. If you are aiming for a 45, this resource might not be enough, but in order to pass the IB, this resource will be worth gold. It is a paid service and is most likely too costly to afford yourself. Therefore, if your school doesn't already have this service, I highly suggest going to your IB coordinator and introducing them to this online textbook that will make your studying easier!

LibGen

Library Genesis (or LibGen) is a search engine for books (and articles) on various topics, which allows free access to content that is otherwise paywalled or not digitized (for example it has the entire library of Elsevier and ScienceDirect – two massive scientific paper publishers). It has textbooks also (university level, but also some IB) ones and over 2 million files – so definitely check it out.

Note: LibGen certainly operates in the gray area of legality so I would be a little cautious when using it (maybe use a VPN).

Sci-Hub

Very similar to LibGen but with a greater emphasis on scientific papers. Again, could be very useful for finding sources for your EE or science lab.

What I usually do is use Google/Google Scholar as a search tool to find papers. When I read the abstract of the paper and think it's relevant, I copy-paste the DOI into sci-hub which swiftly provides me with the full PDF of the entire paper.

These two websites are extremely helpful, especially for EEs when you can really study the exact methodologies and findings of research papers, rather than just general statements. When you go to university, you will be using these a lot so might as well get to grips now.

VPN

If you are for some reason locked out of these two sites, it may be because your country/internet service provider has blocked your access to these sites. In that case, you may wish to install a VPN client, with servers from this site:

https://www.vpngate.net/en/#LIST .

Click on the config file/connect guide in the boxes of the server and follow the instructions on how to use VPN; the instructions are fairly straightforward, comment/message me if you have any questions (preferably comment).

You are now probably questioning if this is ethical. But I genuinely believe knowledge, one of the most important things in the world, should not be behind the paywall of some publisher/licensing company, contrary to many things in the free market.

University books

Especially useful for your EEs, it's good to have some pdfs of first-year university books on your desktop. The reason is that there's only so much that can fit in the IB program, so sometimes the explanation given to us may be insufficient and that's okay. However, if you're one of the "I remember when I really understand" kids, it might be helpful to from time to time spend 20 minutes reading a deeper dive into this topic. It also sometimes helps you in finding inspiration for your EE topic. Another way is watching a recorded lecture course on YouTube if you comprehend information better this way. Although, don't lose focus. In the end, you are tested on the syllabus.

Managebac

ManageBac is the leading planning, assessment and reporting platform for the IB continuum. It is used by nearly 80% of Diploma candidates. It was founded in 2006 by a bunch of ex-IB students to transition schools off paper onto a curriculum-focused learning platform.

If your school doesn't use it already – we highly suggest you lobby them to make the switch as it does alleviate a lot of paperwork and problems.

Paradox of Choice

On the one hand, I am extremely envious of the amount of resources available to modern IB students in comparison to the handful of things we had back in 2007 when I was a student. On the other hand, it does seem as if IB resources have reached a critical point and now there is oversaturation and lots of crap out there.

You need to be very careful with your time (and your wallet) regarding how you approach resources. Identify which ones are the most valuable (and websites like ibresources.org can help you greatly with this) and then stick to those.

Two years is not enough time to go through every possible resource on top of doing all your IB duties. You need to be very efficient with your time, so please keep this in mind when you are looking for new avenues of resources. Your teachers will often know where the best stuff is, so don't hesitate to ask them.

Memes

IB meme pages are a nice distraction – but don't waste too much time going through them. If they stress you out, then avoid.

For most people, however, they provide some nice comic relief.

> **Pro Tip:** On Instagram, follow @smart.ib.memes for the best IB memes, and @smart.ib.resources for daily resource tips!

CHAPTER 8

HOW (NOT) TO USE CHAT GPT

'When do we consider it cheating?'

This chapter might take you by surprise, but it is highly relevant in today's technologically advanced world. Chat GPT has been around since late 2022, and really increased in popularity in 2023. The introduction of this new AI tool has changed the academic world: for both students and teachers. With the rise of Chat GPT came a flood of worry amongst teachers of the new possibilities of cheating with this tool. A main concern was whether or not plagiarism detectors, like Turnitin, would be able to detect if the essay was written by AI or not; in other words, cheating had supposedly been brought to a whole new level.

Now that Chat GPT has been around for over a year, a lot of these concerns are being accompanied by the view that AI will become part of our everyday lives, and that we must adapt programmes to work around this. Plagiarism detectors have since been refined, and yes, if your essay is written by Chat GPT, this will definitely be detected (don't even try it).

I want to dedicate this chapter to explaining to you how, or how not, to use chat GPT. This might strike you as a surprise, since most teachers often preach that using AI is a form of cheating. And this is true. The IB has posted an official statement on their stance regarding the use of Chat GPT. In summary, they acknowledge that "artificial intelligence (AI) technology will become part of our everyday lives" and that they are seeking to "adapt and transform our educational programmes and assessment practices so that students can use these new AI tools ethically and effectively". Essentially, IB is not planning to ban the use of this software but does expect that any use of the software is adequately cited, like any other source. This aligns with their academic integrity policy, since any work produced by AI is not your own. Although this might sound like great news to the fanatic Chat GPT users, keep in mind that citing Chat GPT might not look as credible. In addition, any essay in the IB that is mainly composed of quotations often doesn't score very high, as it shows a lack of critical thinking and personal analysis.

Personally, I have seen students try and use Chat GPT to write IB essays. After having read these essays, I quickly understood that despite how amazing Chat GPT seems, it will never fully understand the criteria, and thus is not able to produce texts to IB standards. People would try and write HL Essays using this tool, and end up with a mostly descriptive text, lacking in-depth evaluation of literary choices, and worst of all: fake quotations. Trust me when I say that Chat GPT essays will not score well, and that if you do use it to write your essay, you will be performing academic dishonesty by breaching the IB's academic integrity policy.

But now, enough about how bad Chat GPT is. I'm sure by now, your teachers have told you that it **is** cheating, and if not, that it has been made clear by me that simply using Chat GPT without proper referencing is a form of plagiarism. Instead, I will now try to show you that Chat GPT can also be used as a helpful tool. When used correctly, AI has the potential to improve us as learners, helping us reach our full potential academically.

For one, the use of Chat GPT for idea generation for IA's is an appropriate use of this tool. It is simply a (better) alternative to a google search, where you can get inspiration for unique IA topics. Finding IA topics is often extremely difficult, especially when your teacher is telling you it should be unique, while also hitting a bunch of other criteria, such as feasibility. I know everyone struggles with this; I personally found it one of the hardest steps of writing the IA. A good topic can determine whether or not you get a good grade (to a certain extent). Therefore, using Chat GPT as inspiration can aid you in the starting steps of writing an IA, giving you ideas you would simply not have thought of yourself.

In addition, the use of Chat GPT to highlight key themes in novels might also prove to be very helpful. Although I still highly recommend you actually **read** the novels assigned to you in your language courses, it might be helpful to have Chat GPT summarize the novel afterwards in terms of key themes. For example, if you're reading *The Narrative of Frederick Douglass*, you might want to delve deeper into dehumanization and the mental effects of slavery. To aid in this process, you could consult Chat GPT to write a brief summary of the presentation of this theme in the text. Then, you can start building off of these key themes and create your own arguments. Do remember to always adequately cite Chat GPT: if you are simply going to be using the AI's arguments, it must be referenced in your works cited.

And lastly, you could simply use Chat GPT as a google search engine when looking for, let's say, an Economics IA article or a research paper to help you with your EE. There are countless other possibilities to using Chat GPT in an ethical manner. The important thing to remember is that the final product produced must be your own. If you doubt whether it is ethical to be using Chat GPT in a certain scenario, you probably shouldn't. Always lean towards the safer side, because being caught for plagiarism, even if accidental, is just about one of the worst things.

OTHER AI RESOURCES

Chat GPT is not the only AI tool out there that can help you in your academic journey. With some quick google searches, I'm sure you could find a multitude of AI resources. I'll start you off by giving some links that have proven useful to me, especially for IA's or EE's.

1. Research Rabbit

This AI tool is an excellent tool for finding sources for your essay or project. This innovative technology allows you to add your sources into a project, whereafter the software will generate an extensive list of similar articles, all of which are from credible journals. This tool might be useful when writing your EE, especially in the sciences or social sciences, where it is crucial that you use credible sources.

2. Chat pdf

This AI tool allows you to determine whether the source you have found is actually useful. Simply put, you upload a pdf to the website, whereafter it will produce a quick summary. In the early stages of research for your EE, this will prove very helpful as it eliminates the need to read long papers that might not help answer your research question.

I highly recommend that if the paper is relevant, you still read it yourself, and draw your own conclusions, as this tool will not engage in any analysis or evaluation.

Revisiondojo.com

If you're tackling the IB and haven't come across Revisiondojo.com yet, you might want to check it out. It's a site put together by a team really keen on helping students. The core of the site? Around 1.8k exam-style questions for all the main IB subjects. Plus, they've thrown in some pretty neat AI tutors and examiners, flashcards, and a mock exam generator.

The kicker? It's all free ... the founders basically use some of their monthly income to fund the project and help as many students as possible! Super cool guys.

To date, they've helped around 150k IB students... and I repeat all completely 100% for FREE!

The AI part is pretty cool – it's like having a robot tutor that teaches you IB stuff, grades your answers, and gives feedback. It's surprisingly on point, and it's got a pretty solid user base already.

Here's what Revisiondojo offers for IB students:

1. AI tutor and examiner: Think of it as your personal robot mentor

2. 2k topic-sorted questions for practice: That's a lot of material to get through

3. Collections: Make your own sets of questions and, if you're feeling generous, share them

4. Question search: For when you need to find something specific

5. Flashcards: Kind of like Quizlet, but tailored for IB

6. Mock Exams: Click a button, get a new practice test

7. Tutoring: If you want a bit more help

Now, everything on Revisiondojo is free, which is pretty sweet. But if you're using it a lot, you might think about their Dojo Plus. It's about $8 a month – basically, the cost of skipping one McDonald's meal. With Dojo Plus, you get unlimited use of their AI, flashcards, question search, and mock exams. And there's a discount code, **SMARTBOOK20**, for 20% off. It's an option if you're really diving deep into the material and want a bit more out of the platform.

CHAPTER 9

HOW TO HACK YOUR GDC AND FORMULA BOOK

'You know you're an IB student when your most prized possession is your Graphing Display Calculator;

The purpose of this chapter is to drill into your head that your graphing display calculator can be a tool of great importance – if you use it correctly and to its full potential. Unfortunately, because there are so many different types of graphing calculators, it will be difficult to go in depth about the secret functions of each one, but I will try to provide a resource where available.

The single best resource that can be found for all basic calculator uses in the IB (Casio fx-9860G, Texas Instruments TI-84 models, Texas Instruments TI-nspire models) is at the Haese Mathematics website. Google 'Haese Mathematics IB calculator instructions' to find a 30-page pdf document that deals extensively with almost everything you need to know about your calculator.

> **Pro Tip**: when answering a trigonometry question, be sure to check that your calculator is set to the correct angle mode – degrees or radians.

There is also another pdf document written by Andy Kemp that deals with the TI-nspire calculator model specifically. You can find it by googling 'IB Mathematics Exam Preparation for Calculator Papers'. The OSC also sells a book that deals with using the TI-Series in IB Mathematics, but you need to purchase this, and it costs 16GBP (bit steep in my honest opinion).

> **Pro Tip:** be familiar with common error messages that your calculator displays

There are also two excellent YouTube videos that are both 40+ mins but are essential viewing if you want to understand how to get the most out of your calculator.

The first is by the HKEXCEL Education Centre and is called 'How to ace your GDC calculator for IB Math', and the other is by mathsl1 channel and is called 'IB Math SL GDC Techniques for Paper 2'. I firmly believe that every IB student should spend time watching these videos as they teach you almost all of the quintessential techniques.

Basic Calculator Tips

1. Graphs displayed on a GDC may be misleading – so make sure that what you see makes sense. Be sure to always check if your window is appropriate- don't always trust zoom fit!

2. Be sure your GDC has new batteries before your final exams.

3. Do not use any calculator notation in your written solutions.

4. Make sure to know all the ins and outs of your calculator: you'll be surprised how helpful it is.

5. When given a function, don't hesitate to graph it in order to quickly find maximum or minimum, or simply just to visualize and better understand the question.

6. On Paper 2, if you solve an equation by means of a graph on your GDC you must provide a clearly labeled sketch of the graph in your work – and indicate exactly what equation you solved on your GDC. It is vital to write down the appropriate mathematical 'set-up' for the computation you will perform on your GDC to obtain all method marks.

7. Even though a GDC is 'required' for Paper 2, do not assume that you will need to use your GDC on every question for Paper 2. Often, you will have to start off a problem with algebra but use your calculator as soon as you can to save time.

8. There will inevitably be some questions on Paper 2 where it will be more efficient to find the answer by using your GDC as opposed to an analytic method. Do not lose valuable time by choosing to answer a question using a tedious analytic method when you could get the answer quickly with your GDC.

9. As you are not allowed a GDC on Paper 1, the questions on this exam will focus on analytic / algebraic 'thinking' solutions. You need to practice these and simple arithmetic and algebraic computations as you won't be able to rely on a GDC.

10. Problems will often ask for exact answers- meaning you can't use your GDC. However, it can be practical to check your solutions using the rounded answer found on your GDC.

> **Pro Tip:** Keep in mind that the Analysis and Approaches course only allows you to use a calculator on paper 2 (and paper 3 if doing HL), while Applications and Interpretations course allows you to always have a calculator.

GDC in IA / EE

If you have the opportunity to use your GDC graphs in your mathematics exploration or mathematics EE (if you are doing one), I would highly suggest this. It looks very impressive, and it shows examiners that you are using the tools at your disposal.

Your calculator should have come with a USB link to your computer and software to extract the graphs / calculations – explore these avenues.

There are also various great graphing calculators online, such as Desmos or Geogebra which can be great tools for mathematics IA's or EE's.

Formula Booklet

I want to take a section of this chapter to also stress the importance of knowing your math, physics or chemistry formula booklet inside out. During exams it is absolutely essential that students know where to quickly find every formula.

Saving time by knowing where to find necessary equations in the data booklet and how to perform shortcuts on the calculator allows for extra time to solve the questions themselves and double-check over work.

You don't want to be spending extra time looking for that one equation only to realize that it's not in the formula booklet, or not know how to perform an essential function on your calculator.

Being familiar with the formula booklet is even more important considering that several useful equations are missing from the formula booklet, and several difficult-to-remember equations are included. Students should therefore know which equations they will need to memorize, and which are easily accessible.

For example, in the HL formula booklet there is the formula for the angle between two vectors, but not between two planes or a vector and a plane.

For Math

Knowing your formula booklet will help you a TON. Losing 3 seconds every time you look for a formula during an exam is a huge mistake. Don't be that kid. Know where the equations are. Trust me. It'll give you the chance for an extra few marks.

For Physics

Your data booklet is your best friend. This is in a similar way to what I wrote about the formula booklet for math but different. The IB Physics data booklet is an asshole. Literally.

They try to trip you up by using different notations here and there. I

Your data booklet is your best friend. Even in physics. However, be wary. The physics formula booklet purposefully will try to trip you up by using different notations here and there. I fell into that trap in my P3 exam. So, make sure you know the tricks of the data booklet because it can save your grades during an exam.

However, the formula booklet can also be viewed as your holy grail. All the formulas are separated based on the unit they belong to, making it easy to use. Additionally, if you know all the variables, it becomes easier to start solving questions that seem gibberish to you at first. Just follow these simple steps:

1. Identify the variable you need to solve for.

2. Write down the information that is given to you in the problem (e.g. mass, time, distance, current, etc.).

3. Find a formula that uses (most) of those variables. You might need to use multiple formulas but work with what you have! If anything, you will still get marks for writing down the right formula.

For Chemistry

I am a lover of formula booklets, but I despise the chemistry formula booklet. Anyone that has seen one knows what I'm talking about: they are almost thicker than this novel. Furthermore, they are confusing.

I recommend asking your teacher to spend a lesson dissecting the formula booklet at some point. There are so many hidden gems in there that I only discovered right before my exams! For example, there are lists of organic compounds, multiple periodic tables displaying various properties, colors of acids and bases in different indicators, and so much more.

I do have to note that for paper 1, you are not allowed access to this formula booklet. You will have to learn a lot of the properties, but then, during your paper 2, you can use your formula booklet to double check something or to find something you simply forgot.

CHAPTER 10

HOW TO ACHIEVE FULL MARKS ON YOUR IA

'You know you're in the IB when you skip school to do your Internal Assessments'

Internal Assessment (IA) is the easiest, most effective and fastest way to get top marks in almost all your subjects. You would have to be extremely silly to ignore that fact.

Try doing some simple math. If we say that, on average, IA takes up roughly 25% of your grade for each subject then that means it takes up ¼ of the maximum grade 7 per subject – nearly two entire points.

Now, this may not seem like much, but when you consider that you have 6 subjects plus the 3 bonus points from TOK/EE – this adds up to 15 points towards your IB diploma. Simply put, from maxing out on your

Internal Assessment and EE/TOK you can get 15 marks even before you step into the examination room.

That's the beauty of it. You have no idea what a comforting feeling it is walking into the exam room knowing you already have 12 – 15 points in the bag.

One must try to remain realistic. No matter how much you have studied, no matter how many past papers you have done, and no matter how well you have grasped the material, what happens on the exam day will to a certain extent be outside of your control.

What if you break an arm, get a stomach virus or become ill during the exam? What if all three happen? What if your co-coordinator makes a mistake and forgets to give you a periodic table for your HL Chemistry exam (as has happened)? What if you just "go blank" when you open your exam and forget all that you have crammed the night before?

I have seen some of the best IB candidates underperform on exam day simply because of bad luck and misfortune.

Another likely scenario is that you are simply not an exam person. I am usually very comfortable with the material, spend plenty of time studying, and usually can answer most questions when asked verbally in a non-exam situation.

However, when the clock is ticking and the pressure is on, I tend to only perform at about 80% of my potential. I am not an "exam person". In fact, I hate examinations because so many factors are outside of your control. There are too many ways in which one can make careless mistakes and mess up. This is not the case with IA.

As I was trying to point out, IA makes up roughly 25% of your grade for each subject. In subjects such as English it amounts to nearly 30% of the grade. So even before you sit your English exam, you are nearly 1/3rd done. This means that if you have done amazingly well on your IA, you already have 2 or 3 marks secured towards your English grade.

It is a very comforting feeling to know that no matter how poorly you perform on your exam, you are almost definitely in the 4 to 7 range – in other words you are comfortably going to pass. This may not mean much to the more ambitious candidates reading this manual. If you are amongst the IB candidates who worry about failing the IB diploma, then this IA stuff can save you.

Now some of you may still need further convincing that Internal Assessment is extremely important. The words 'lab report', 'economic commentary' and 'IO' are so often used in the same breath as the word 'homework' that students forget to realize the importance of IA. The points add up, and before you know it, it might be too late to go back and capitalize on your IA marks.

Let's think about this logically. The assessment is usually given a week or even a few weeks in advance. For bigger assignments, such as the Extended Essay you have substantially more time to prepare. You are given weeks to complete something that will account for a generous fraction of your final grade.

Now contrast this with the final examinations, which will usually take up the remaining 60% - 75% of your final grade. The exam duration per subject is rarely more than 6 or 7 hours. Those few hours will decide what you will get for the remaining portion of your grade. Would it not make sense then to work relentlessly on maximizing your mark for the IA simply because you are given so much more time and space? The final examination goes by in a blink of an eye whereas you are given an abundance of time to work on your IA. Once you realize this, you will make sure your IAs are as flawless as possible.

> **Pro Tip:** get started on your IAs as early as possible. Find out from each teacher when they will officially assign them.

You are given weeks, if not months, to decide nearly a fourth of your grade, and then you are given two or three hours to decide the remaining three-fourths. It would be foolish to put in less effort for the IA then the actual examinations. They are practically handing you these marks. No matter how poorly you know the material, or how poorly you perform on examinations, nearly anyone can ace their Internal Assessment – especially given the advice provided further in this chapter.

So, if you are one of those people who tend to underperform in examinations and simply can't bother studying, you absolutely need to take full advantage of the IA. It baffles me as to why so many students fail to see this loophole. Even the top IB candidates often focus so much on learning the material and doing well in the actual exams that they lose track of the fact that IA also counts towards the final grade.

With regards to the order of importance for IB-related daily matters, I would suggest the following rank: 1) Internal Assessment, 2) revision for tests, 3) homework. This means that if you have an economics commentary due the next day and a test as well, you need to finish and polish the commentary before you even start thinking about revising for the test. Tests will come and go, but you will have few opportunities to redo your Internal Assessments.

All the labs, coursework, portfolios and papers that make up your IA are of far greater importance than any test or homework assignment that you must do. Yes, your trimester grade may suffer. Yes, the teacher may get on your back for not doing the homework. Nonetheless, you need to keep a voice in the back of your head telling you that "at the end of the day, small tests and homework won't give me my 7's, the IB assessment will." Word of caution: if you have teachers who heavily rely on homework and tests as predicted grade markers, you will need to reconsider this advice.

Also, many students use IAs as an excuse to stop doing homework. This is a bad idea because homework is not 'skipped'. It only piles up and comes back to haunt you. We all know that there are two categories of homework...the necessary kind and the unnecessary kind. For example, necessary homework would be a Chemistry worksheet on Organic structures that is marked by your teacher as an assignment. Unnecessary homework would be a stack of 500 equation-balancing problems (you can do this slowly, especially if your teacher isn't collecting it).

The beauty behind Internal Assessment is that literally anyone, of any academic ability, can get top marks. This is great news for those of you who do not plan on studying much for the exams, or who are terrified of test-taking. All you need to do is spend an incredible amount of time constantly improving and upgrading your assignment. I have seen some pretty daft IB students ace their assignments simply because they spent day and night perfecting them. Although they may not have been academically gifted, at least they realized the potential impact that IA could have on their grades – and in that sense, they are geniuses.

It doesn't matter whether you are "smart". You simply need to be ruthless when it comes to completing your IA assignments. Follow the guidelines that I provide in this book for each subject on how to maximize your IA. If you do that, then regardless of how good or bad you think you are at a certain subject, you will be able to get a "handicap" of +2 on your final grade before you sit the exam.

You need to become the King (or Queen) of IA in your class. All the other students will be in awe as you get 19/20 back for your Math IA or a near full mark for your Economics portfolio. They may say you are wasting your time aiming for the perfect IA assessment, but when you get your final grades back you will be laughing at them. You need to strive to have the best coursework possible.

I remember a few months before final examinations some teachers would announce whose work was getting sent off to be moderated. Now, I don't know how the system works inside out, but I have a feeling that for IA the IBO demands that a good distribution of student work is sent off. In other words: the top assignments, the average assignments and the assignments at the lower end of the grading scale. I would look around the class to see who else was having their work sent off, and immediately I could tell that my work was part of the "top assignments" (our teacher never told us whose work got selected). This took a lot of stress off the final examinations. It is an incredible feeling when you are revising to know that you are 25% closer to getting your 7s.

Getting top marks in your IA is not an easy task. Then again, neither is getting 7's in your examinations. The key difference is that whereas with the exams you are given a few hours to show your worth, the IA timeline is much more generous. You will need to work late nights, weekends, and holidays to get top marks for your IA. In fact, you would probably work just as hard (if not harder) a few weeks prior to your exams, so I don't see why this would be such a daunting task.

You need to develop a habit of wanting to strive for perfection in all your externally moderated IAs. Treat this as being just as important as the actual exam, or even more so. I want you to start feeling extremely disappointed if you are getting back labs/commentaries/portfolios that are below a grade 6.

Not only should you be getting 7's, but you should also be getting high 7's. Keep in mind that what your teacher thinks you deserve is not the final grade. It will be moderated and probably hiked up or down a few notches. You should therefore make sure to leave a little room for change when you are told your predictions.

Given the fact that you are reading this book, I think I can safely assume that you are not the naturally gifted IB diploma student who is predicted to get a 45. You may struggle getting 6's or even 5's on your school tests. At the same time, you may be a student who is borderline failing the diploma program and is anticipating the worst when the final examinations come around. In either case, this advice about IA is of equal importance. IA can turn a failing IB diploma grade of 15 to a 30. Or a 30 to a 45. The important thing is that you take this advice and follow it through.

I firmly believe that if a student maxes out on his/her IA, then it is nearly impossible to fail the IB diploma. You will get somewhere around 15 marks for your assignments alone (given that you get all 3 bonus marks), which leaves just about 10 more marks from your actual examination. I have yet to meet a person that cannot scrape 10 marks on their actual examinations. If you maximize your IA marks, then you are entering a stress-free world of examinations. Instead of deciding where you will be on a scale of 0 to 45, you now can estimate your final grade on a scale of 15 to 45.

I know I am getting repetitive, but you need to drill this into your head. You need to strive for perfection on your Internal Assessment. Do that and you are one step, one giant leap, closer to getting what you want from your IB diploma. Don't be ignorant, realize the power of IA marks and the effect that they can have on your final grade.

You don't know how much you will hate yourself when you find out that the reason you missed out on getting your dream grade of 45 was due to a poorly done IA that dragged you down to a 44 overall. Or how about finding out that the only reason you failed IB was because you "forgot" to hand in an Economics commentary, and this dragged you down below 24 marks. Be smart: milk the IA for all that it is worth.

It's a miracle that a notoriously "rigorous" program such as the IB diploma program would have nearly 25% of the final score decided on a non-exam basis. You are lucky that final grades aren't based entirely on your ability to perform well in exams as is the case in many other high school programs worldwide.

This provides a great opportunity for those of you who are hard-working and intelligent yet lack that cutting edge when it comes to examinations. Take full advantage of this – it won't be long before the IB starts to diminish the importance of Internal Assessment (they already have over the last decade) and add greater value to the actual examinations.

Students stress about final exams, but in this case you'll have got a whole bunch of grades before you even get to them. This has an extraordinary implication for you. Imagine an exam system in which they ask you whatever you want to study, let you decide how to study and even let you write some of the questions.

This is basically the IB system: between 20% and 40% of your grades you can get from work that you can write, check, triple-check, get friends and families to advise you, change work, mark yourself, and work out certainly what mark the examiner will give.

IAs are the only aspect of IB that you have real 'control' over. You get to write your own questions and come up with your own answers. As mentioned, most IAs also make up at least 20% of your final grade and do make the difference between 6s and 7s.

For example, if you got a low 5 on your Math IA, you'd need to get 95+% on the final exam to get a 7; if you got a 7 already, you can make do with about 80%. That 15%, as we all know, is a huge difference. Don't treat IAs like projects in middle school. They are imperative and, as I believe, designed to help you gain marks before the final exams.

With regards to time management, I'm sure that nobody wants to hand in a crap IA. It's just that we are sometimes forced to that point by outside pressures, i.e. lack of time. What many students need to understand is that time is 'created', not 'found'.

Nature does not give you any time, you need to squeeze it out by yourself. Confucius probably said something about time being like 'water in a sponge'. Unfortunately, time in the IB world is more like 'maple syrup in a sponge' and is hard to eke out. It is nevertheless possible to maintain high standards on your IAs.

General IA Advice

You need to choose the right question. This is where many candidates fail, as they are over-ambitious and bite off more than they can chew. Choose a question that you're interested in, but which also pertains to the course. Yes, IB is about learning, but also about passing. Also, get advice on your question ASAP. Even when the teacher has just announced the IA. Brainstorm as fast as possible and ask for a quality check on your ideas. This saves you lots of time in the long run. A good research question can make or break your IA.

'Why do work when you can get others to do it for you?' is an age-old technique; some people call it 'leverage'. Unfortunately, getting your teachers to help doesn't mean you can just laze at home and do nothing. You need to make life easy for them - make plans, make time to see them, organize everything, be ready when they ask you questions. If you keep up a disciplined image, they will be lots more likely to take you seriously. For IAs...they can only mark one draft but go see them in their office and make them read over the edited parts again and again. They want you to get a 7.

Some teachers are quite unfriendly/unknowledgeable and so you don't want to see them. That's alright too. You just need to replicate the 'teacher' process at home. You need to set goals for yourself. Don't say 'I need to get this done before July because it is the deadline'. You should tell yourself, "The first draft is due to myself/IB gods on 15 June." Get a friend to help you with accountability if needed - make sure to return the favor.

Squeezing out time is a special art. You need to look at your current life and do a 'time budget'. What are you spending time on? What can you cut out? It's like calorie counting but with minutes.

> **Pro Tip:** create your own IA deadlines well in advance of the school set ones – this way you will have plenty of time to work on your draft

I know these measures sound quite 'hardcore' but...you will thank yourself when the final exams arrive, and you know that you don't have to get an impossible score in order to reach your goal. This can actually give you a major confidence boost when it matters the most. Spread out your suffering. Piling up IAs are like cars. When you have an accident on the highway, they tend to pile up.

When faced with a developing or fully developed pile, the first thing you need to do is be honest with yourself. Take a survey of the situation and write down all that you must do. Then do these as a priority.

Many students confuse 'priority' with 'preference'. Yes, doing your History IA is more fun than making graphs for your Math IA. But if your Math IA is due next week and the History IA is due next month, don't even think about doing History first. If you're having too much fun with a pileup on your plate, chances are...you're not prioritizing.

You can also try a 'war of attrition' against your work, but this is more of a pre-emptive measure. Basically, do a bit of work at every available opportunity. Social lives are important but...if you need that extra 20 minutes, man up, skip recess, and do your chemistry assignment. That 20 minutes can then be saved at home for EE writing purposes. Basically, every second counts.

With regards to sleep, you don't need to stay up till 3am or pull an all-nighter. Most people go to school from 8am to 3pm or similar hours. What are you doing from 4pm to 10pm?

That's a full 6 hours for you to get some stuff done. You have months to do your IAs. The rest of your time can be used for study, recreation, and much-needed sleep. You don't feel it, especially if you're hopped up on caffeine, but your work quality is going to be lower after a whole day of school and not sleeping.

Another key tip: get your hands on the subject reports. These are reports where the examiners explain what exactly was good or bad in last year's IAs (and exams) and give a whole section of advice to teachers and students on how to do better. Your teacher should have them, and you should seek these out.

> **Pro Tip:** go through the Teacher Support Material and highlight carefully what you think is important in the sample graded IAs – do this for the good IAs and the bad IAs so you know what to do and what to avoid doing.

TOP 10 GENERAL IA TIPS

1. Pick a unique topic

The IB seems to be a bit obsessed with originality in your IA work. Examiners don't like to read the same thing over and over again. Of course, for you all the topics will seem 'new' since it's your first time doing an IA. Do a little search online and avoid common topics that seem to get done every day. Try to pick something that's a little interesting. However, I must disclaim that in a lot of the subject areas, especially the sciences, most feasible topics have been done before. Thus, maybe try and build off of some ideas you have found online: could you change the way you measure the dependent variable, or could you change the independent variable all together? Don't stress too much about making the topic completely unique, but don't do the most mainstream topic either.

2. Don't force personal engagement

If you read over all the criteria, you will know that personal engagement is a big factor. The examiners will want to see evidence of this. This can be in the form of a unique methodology, or insightful extensions and analysis. However, please, don't try to force personal engagement by writing things like 'I am really passionate about x / I love x' because examiners are not morons, they will see right through this. Try to write something that seems organic and natural. Don't force it.

3. Try not to make shit up

Integrity is an important part of the IB program. If your experiment or survey didn't get you the results you were looking for, perhaps try to do it over again. Make sure you reference everything properly and don't have made up sources. If you get caught, you will be f*cked. Getting perfect results is less important than that. It is still possible to get a good grade, even if your results don't perfectly show what you wanted them to: it's all about the analysis and evaluation!

4. Format matters

All the things that make up the format (table numbers, fonts, diagrams) are important too. Also having proper references and citations. Make your report look pretty and professional (here is where it also helps to look at past successful IAs and how they are formatted). Presentation really matters – you want your IA to look like a professional piece of work and not some crappy middle school project.

Keep in mind that there are significant format differences across the groups. A Language and Literature IA will not look the same as a chemistry IA. Be sure to read all the requirements, and parameters, such as word count, page count (often only for scientific IA's), etc. These are easy points you don't want to lose.

5. Label all of your diagrams

If you include a picture – make sure the picture is i) significant ii) important for the examiner to see and iii) properly labeled. Having a picture with no labels will lose you marks as the examiner tries to figure out why that thing is there.

6. Proofread everything

Make sure your math is correct and there are no mistakes in your text. Even the slightest mistake in any IA can cost you dearly.

7. Quality over quantity

This might seem a bit cliché, but it really makes sense in the context of your IA. It's much better to have a 7-8 page IA that's dense with good stuff than a 12+ page one which is filled with bullshit. You don't want to ramble repetitively. Examiners hate that.

8. Use references and give societal relevance

Why does your topic matter in the grade scheme of things? The IB loves to see some real-world applicability and how your IA relates to society.

9. Weave your knowledge into your analysis

Don't just put a bunch of textbook info into your IA wherever you please. You need to learn how to weave it into your analysis and only talk about it where it really matters. You want to demonstrate your knowledge, but you don't want your IA to be a textbook. It is so important to go further than just stating knowledge; to get top marks you must engage in active evaluation and analysis.

10. Explain everything clearly.

Assume the person reading your IA isn't familiar with the topic. Explain everything in short succinct sentences. Don't overcomplicate things.

Getting a Second Opinion

Once you think you have 'finished' your IA, it will help to get a second opinion so have your friends look over and mark it as if they were an examiner. Make sure you do the same for them. Remember, you are not competing against each other and in fact, it benefits both of you to have a class where all the IAs are of excellent quality.

It is NOT recommended to ask for IB kids on forums to proofread your IA on the internet. You should keep your IA private because these things do get copied if you leave it out there for the world to see. Please don't submit your IA anywhere online until after you have received your IB diploma.

IA Proofreading Services

There is now an abundance of professional services that guarantee to look over and improve your IA. Should you do this?

I'm a bit on the fence about this. On the one hand, lots of kids are getting their personal tutors to help them out with their IA work. On the other hand, it borders on academic malpractice. Certainly, services where you send in your IA and they just send it back to you would be deemed as plagiarism because it's no longer your own work. You need to be careful, and you need to know whether what you are doing is okay or not.

I know for a fact that there is a considerable amount of kids every year who consult these services. Personally, I would never consider it because I always believe that *I* can do better and that only *I* know the secrets of getting a top mark in my IA. My advice is to be very cautious if considering paying someone to 'help' with your IA, and probably avoid it.

These services are rarely of high quality, and even if they are it will often be obvious that you've used an external source. Teachers can notice changes in writing style., and who knows if these services are using additional sources without citing, or even copying directly from websites?.

Top Tip: avoid using shady IA proofreading services. You can get more timely and effective feedback by swapping with a friend and reading through each other's. Perhaps find another teacher and get them to read through it, too, and give feedback.

Teacher Support Material

The TSM (outlined in greater detail in the chapter on past papers) actually includes very useful information regarding the IA so it is imperative that you get your hands on it. For example, for the sciences, the last part of the document has a section on 'practical work' and a chapter on new IA criteria. There are also 10 pre-assessed labs. This is the most useful part of the material and is certainly worth looking at in detail. The TSM material is organized into 'student work', 'annotated student work' and 'moderators' comments' – so you can see exactly what high scoring IAs did that others did not do! It is **extremely useful** stuff.

> **Pro Tip:** search for the latest Teacher Support Material to get access to moderated IAs with comments (best bet is to search r/IBO)

IA deadlines

The following table lists these components and the dates by which the work must be uploaded (May candidates / November candidates) on the IBIS eCoursework system.

Subject/Component	Latest arrival date
Extended essay	15 March/15 September
Theory of knowledge essay	15 March/15 September
Language A: literature written assignment	15 March/15 September
Language A: language and literature written tasks	15 March/15 September
Literature and performance SL written coursework	15 March/15 September
Language B written assignment	15 March/15 September
Language ab initio written assignment	15 March/15 September
Visual arts: comparative study	30 April/30 October
Visual arts: process portfolio	30 April/30 October
Music: musical links investigation	30 April/30 October

Subject/Component	Latest arrival date
Film: independent study and presentation	30 April/30 October
Dance: composition and analysis	30 April/30 October
Dance: dance investigation	30 April/30 October
Theatre: solo theatre piece (HL only); director's notebook and research presentation (SL and HL)	30 April/30 October
Language A: literature SL school-supported self-taught oral examination audio recording	7 May/7 November

Do note that your school may have internal deadlines different from these deadlines, and your school may reject late submission of work. This is particularly true of IAs, where the final uploaded work needs to have teachers' comments alongside it.

CHAPTER 11

HOW TO USE PAST PAPERS

'There is no such thing as too many past papers questions'

If you have been reading this guide carefully then you should know just how much I have stressed the importance of past papers.

Let me put it to you this way. If Internal Assessment takes around 25% of final IB grade, then your experience and practice with past papers could determine around *half* of what your final IB grade will be.

The remaining 25% is down to a mixture of determination, natural academic ability and luck. Simply put, past papers are imperative when it comes to passing your examinations.

Once again, to truly understand the power of past papers, we need to think logically. The syllabi for most subjects have been written many years ago. The IB examinations are written to test your knowledge and grasp of the syllabus material.

Thus, there is only so much that they can possibly ask. If you carefully look through past papers, repeatedly you are bound to see major similarities.

> **Pro Tip:** Do EVERY past paper. When you take exams, you will be surprised about how many questions you have seen before, or similar styles of questions.

Of course, the degree of similarity will vary across subjects, but nonetheless it is a fair statement to make that questions often repeat themselves. Think of it this way: there is a set amount of information you need to learn, and the IBO wants to test your knowledge with respect to this information. Every year they will ask questions to test this knowledge. Surely there are only so many ways they can test you. Eventually they start to run out of original questions.

Luckily for you, this has already happened. Look at the grade above you; they were arguably worse off. Similarly, the grade below you is better off. Why? Because yet another year of modern IB examinations has gone by. That means another set of past paper questions and markschemes has been made available. Consider yourself lucky that you have so much access to past papers and markschemes because ten years ago this was certainly not the case.

At the top UK universities (including Oxford and Cambridge) you will find it impossible to get your hands on any markschemes. Past examinations are usually available (and even that can be a hassle), but mark schemes are non-existent.

The reasoning for this is quite simple to understand. The universities don't want students to simply digest the mark schemes without learning the material properly. It levels out the playing field and makes the competition for top marks fiercer. Luckily for you, the IB does not have this policy. Past papers and markschemes are recommended by the IBO and made available – albeit sometimes at a monetary cost.

Where do I get them?

The simple answer to this is anywhere you can. If you are amongst the lucky few then it can be the case that your school has an abundance of money and resources and will readily supply you with past papers and markschemes because they know how valuable they are. On the other hand, you may be at a school that lacks the financial muscle to buy these for students and is honest enough to not download and photocopy any.

Nonetheless the first place you need to go to is your school. Your teachers, the library, your IB coordinator – basically anyone that might be able to help you. At some schools, students have access to nearly all available past examinations, however the teachers may restrict what they give out because they may use them as future mock examinations. Even if the papers are covered in cobwebs and in a dusty old closet, make sure to get them out and look for more.

If that route fails, your next best option would probably be to go to the one place that has the answers to almost everything; the Internet (please refer to my chapter on the Internet for all the information that you need).

Be aware of a few things first though. First of all, the IB strictly forbids any persons to host past papers and markschemes on the Internet (aside from the official store) and they regularly hunt down and threaten anyone who does with a takedown. If you are lucky enough to find a website that does host past papers then it's unlikely to be there in a few weeks' time.

Second, be careful with some websites as there can be a lot of dodgy ones that host past papers.

Third, (and I will reiterate this time and time again throughout the book because it is of immense importance): once you have found all the past papers you need, DOWNLOAD everything and store it on an external drive (hop on Amazon and you can buy a little USB thumb drive with 64GB for next to nothing – that will host all your files!). These websites really come and go, and they tend to go down whenever you need them most (like right before exams).

Pro Tip: once you are on an IB resources website with documents that you need – **DOWNLOAD EVERYTHING** that is applicable to your subjects and store it offline because that website will go down when you need it most.

The last option you have is the most hassle-free: buying past papers and markschemes directly from the IBO website. Now, don't get me wrong. I am against spending any more money on what is already a very expensive program. Nor do I understand why the IB would charge students more for additional "information."

What I strongly recommend you do is round up ten or so classmates who are interested in getting past papers and markschemes for a particular subject. If you each chip in, then together you can buy a copy from the official IBO past paper provider. Once you have all the papers you need you can share the papers between each other because they will be made available in a downloadable pdf format. Additionally, once you're done with your exams you can sell the papers off to the grade below.

> **Pro Tip:** learn to share everything with your classmates – past papers included. You guys are all in this together and you shouldn't compete against each other.

All in all, you should never be spending more money on past papers than you would on a textbook – and past papers are technically far more valuable than any textbook (in my honest opinion).

You need to get your hands on these papers, one way or another.

How many?

Although I would usually urge you to do more past papers in rough rather than one or two thoroughly, this approach also has its limitations. A good general approximation that I recommend is doing at least five years' worth of examinations (both May and November papers). This adds up to ten separate examinations – which is a considerable amount of practice.

Of course, this will vary from subject to subject. For example, for Group 1 topics, there is very little point in looking at more than 3 years' worth of exams whereas for HL Mathematics you wouldn't do yourself any harm working through ten years of examinations if you really want that 7.

A good rule to follow is to make sure you do enough past papers so that you start seeing repeat questions. Only then will you become comfortable and familiar with what the questions ask you to do.

> **Pro Tip:** if you get a specific question wrong, then go back and find as many possible versions as possible of that question. This is why the questionbanks are useful as they let you search. Look for patterns in how the question is asked

Avoid going too far back into the database if you know there has been a serious change in syllabus/exam structure. For example, the HL Economics Paper 1 exam used to be multiple choice questions a decade ago. There is little point in looking at too many of those multiple-choice papers because you no longer have to sit such a paper. That being said, just because there has been a slight change in the method of examination doesn't mean you should ignore the papers totally.

There are few feelings worse than having just sat an exam where one of the questions was incredibly similar to a past paper that you decided not to do. I highly doubt you can feel overly confident going into an examination if you haven't taken your chance to do all the past papers you could get your hands on (or at least glance over them properly). Make sure you don't have this regret – do enough past papers.

Past Papers vs. Markschemes

Some of you may be asking what's more important, the past paper or the markscheme? They are both of equal importance and you can't really have one without the other. There is no point in running through paper after paper if you have no way to check if your answers are even remotely correct.

Similarly, you cannot just flick through random answers in the markschemes if you have no idea what the question was asking (unless, that is, the mark scheme has the questions included).

Ultimately, you need to have both the past paper and the markscheme for every examination that you are interested in. You will undoubtedly spend more time with the markscheme than you will with the past paper because you will want to see exactly what examiners are looking for. Nonetheless, get the past papers as well in case you want to do a practice examination or want to get a "feel" for the structure of the exam.

How do I "do" the past paper?

Contrary to what your teachers may have told you, it is not a crime to have the markscheme with you whilst you are answering questions from a past paper (sometimes!). This is one of the best forms of revision and is a method that is severely underused by students.

Ideally, you would want to complete each paper properly in the time set and only then get out the markscheme to see what mistakes you made. But we don't live in an ideal world. You don't have the time to sit 3-hour mock examinations for tens of papers in 6 different subjects and then go through each one with the markscheme (but if you somehow do then by all means do this instead!). Your revision doesn't even really start until all the assessment is sent off so you will at best have a month or two of pure revision.

So, what is the best thing to do once you have obtained the papers and the markschemes? Well, it will largely depend on you and what works for you individually. Personally, I found that for subjects such as Economics and

Geography, I needed the markscheme near me as I was answering the questions from the past papers. I would have a scrap piece of paper next to me as well, glance at the question, jot down a rough answer, and then check with the markscheme what I missed out.

> **Pro Tip:** I'd urge you to avoid doing extremely recent papers. I saved up last year's November papers for solving 2-3 weeks before the actual exam. This gave me the most accurate indication of what I might end up scoring in the actual exam.

For Mathematics and Physics however, I found that by looking at the answers before I fully finished the question, I was cheating myself. As a result, I usually kept the markscheme away until I was totally stumped or found some sort of answer.

The key thing to keep in mind is that you need to be constantly writing. Don't fool yourself into thinking you can go and lie down on your couch, past paper in one hand, markscheme in the other. Your revision needs to be active.

> **Pro Tip:** try to replicate the exam room scenario as best as possible when doing past papers – quiet room, no distractions, clock..

From my experience, I found that writing bullet-point scrap answers for past paper questions helped me learn the material much more than simply pondering over the answer and glancing at the markscheme.

Remember what you are ultimately aiming for: to understand the material and be able to answer the question to the examiner's expectations. Your work with past papers and markschemes should make you feel more confident. If you pick up a past paper and are in total fear of what they ask, then clearly you are not yet prepared.

Don't underestimate the power of this technique. Mark schemes are everything when it comes to scoring 7's in your subjects. Not only do they provide model answers but there is also a clear breakdown for the examiners, so they know when to award marks. You have at your disposal everything that makes for a perfect examination.

Pro Tip: Get fast - you need to be able to work through exams quickly and have ample time to look over your answers and revisit questions you may have left out, and doing past questions is the best way to do that.

The closer you get to this perfection, the closer you will get to that grade 7. You will learn what it takes to make your paper worthy of a high mark. Learn to speak the examiner's language. Look for keywords and phrases, memorize certain model definitions, and learn to give them what they are looking for.

By the time I was midway through my exams I had past papers and markschemes all over the place along with the model answers I wrote myself. The coffee table, the bedroom, the bathroom, the kitchen – everything and everywhere was covered with past papers.

When you surround yourself with this information, you are less likely to forget it. By constantly consulting the past papers and markschemes you ensure that you will not be surprised by anything that could come up in the real examination.

SL/HL

Some of you may wonder whether there is any sense in going through past papers at a level which you do not necessarily do. This is at times fine if you are a Higher-Level student looking to get a greater grasp of the questions and the syllabus, but I would not recommend that you go through Higher Level papers if you are a Standard Level student.

> **Pro Tip:** start a spreadsheet and track your progress with past papers so you can see which questions types you are struggling with (also it might give you a clue which questions might come up if you notice a pattern)

You will not be "challenging yourself". You will probably just get confused and frightened because you won't be able to answer most of the questions. For example, I avoided looking at HL Physics papers because I found the SL ones challenging and adequate enough. That being said, I got too familiar with most of the HL Geography papers available, so I started to go over a few SL papers (which was ok because the gap between SL and HL was not that great).

Use your common sense and don't waste your time doing papers that are of no use to you.

Other Resources

Aside from past papers and markschemes, there are at least four more resources that are severely underrated by IB students. I can tell you from my first-hand experience that understanding how to utilize these resources will allow you to study smarter.

1. Subject Guides

Every subject you do should have a so-called 'subject guide' which is a publication intended to guide the planning, teaching, and assessment for educators to deliver the course. The subject guide is usually a massive official document that covers everything you need to know about the subject. It explains the nature of the subject, the course, and the syllabus. Most importantly, it clarifies the assessment that you undertake

I recommend that this is the first thing that you read **even before you begin your subject**, and you continuously refer back to it throughout the two years since it's very helpful to know what you are studying – especially as far as how and why you are assessed.

2. Syllabus

Perhaps this is not that underrated since everyone tells you constantly to use the syllabus, yet you would be surprised how many students overlook the syllabus. The syllabus basically contains everything you need to know. It's kind of a giant 'cheat sheet' for all the information you need to acquire. For exam revision, you should ensure that you know every single point on there.

The syllabus is most helpful for subjects like math and science, and also economics and geography.

3. Teacher Support Material (TSM)

This is material that is given to teachers which provides guidance for their marking. It's based on past student's sample work in their IAs and it shows exactly where they have lost or gained marks based on the assessment rubric. It can help you identify and contextualize the rubric and truly understand how to earn the high marks

Since it's an official document, it's also a great resource to draw inspiration from.

4. Examiners Subject Report

The examiner's report is an extremely useful document. Reading it and acting upon it are paramount to ensuring good examination results. This is honestly the best resource and one which 90% of students are not even aware exists.

The reports usually come out 3 months after examinations

So, what does it contain? The examiner's report contains a very detailed breakdown of the examination session. It details the overall percentages needed to achieve the respective grades at HL and SL as well as a paper-by-paper breakdown of the marks needed to achieve a particular grade in each paper. It also includes this for the IA. It can be quite revealing as to how (relatively) high or low some of these grade boundaries are.

> **Pro Tip:** don't underestimate the importance of the examiner's report – it is as important, if not more, than past papers and markschemes!

Secondly, it includes an extremely thorough analysis of each question in every examination paper. It is often quite reassuring to find that the questions you would struggle with are also questions that students throughout the world also struggle with.

It also includes recommendations for teaching. Points that the chief examiner feels that we are doing well and not so well. It is not just a case of looking at which questions were answered poorly.

The chief examiner often picks up on common mistakes or misconceptions made by students (that may have come about through poor teaching) – take this as good, positive advice from the chief examiner. It is important as different countries/ different systems do have different ways of teaching or different interpretations of similar points.

Finally, the examiner's report gives really detailed advice of the IA.

Pro Tip: The examiner's report with respect to IA can give you heaps of information as to what the moderators have been instructed to look for – and this can be priceless advice.

IB Past Papers Petition

Granting students access to the past papers has been a mission of mine for the past decade. So much so that I started a petition that asks the IBO to release all the materials for all students. I believe this is the only fair thing to do and I explain why in this change.org petition, which I have linked here:

www.change.org/p/international-baccclaureate-organization-make-past-papers-and-markschemes-freely-available-smartib

You can also find it by searching change.org for the 'IB past papers petition'.

Please, if you could read the petition and sign it, it would be one step closer to getting all future students' access to these essential materials.

Concluding Remarks

The point of this chapter was to make you appreciate the potential that past papers and markschemes offer. The most successful IB candidates nowadays heavily rely on past examination questions simply because it is an unbeatable strategy. Your teachers will probably disagree that learning from past papers and markschemes is a more effective study technique than learning from textbooks/notes, but they have not done the exams themselves.

Trust me on this one. Unless you have done absolutely as many past papers as you possibly can you will not be ready to sit the examinations and get that grade 7. I cannot stress this enough, but I trust you have enough good judgment to see the logic behind this.

CHAPTER 12

HOW TO REVISE LIKE A PRO

'A wise senior once told me that you can do all of your IB revision in the last week before your exams. He is a proud member of his safety college now.'

Preparing for the final exams can be a daunting task. Once the examination timetable is published, your first exam date will remain cemented in your mind.

Although there are hundreds of ways to revise for the examinations, many are largely ineffective and far too time consuming. In this chapter I will give you some general guidelines for how to best revise for your final exams.

The Long Haul

I can't stress enough how important it is to stay on top of your work throughout the years.

Missing a unit here and there will cause you tremendous stress as you're trying to cram it into your brain right before the final exam. Take advantage of the internal exams that schools provide you with, such as end of year exams. Most people will dismiss these exams; after all, they don't count towards your final grade. DON'T DO THIS! By revising for these exams, as well as mocks, you are making your future self VERY happy. In most classes, this will consist of taking relevant notes (no need for the extra fluff that is often taught in textbooks) in an actual notebook. Think about the end goal: the information must be relevant to the syllabus and help you with the final exam. And yes, I said handwritten notes, so no laptop! It is scientifically proven that you will retain the information better if you write it down. And it is even more beneficial to use colors and highlighters, but not everyone is interested in making their notes look pretty, and that's okay too. Your notes must help YOU! If you don't think you'll remember the acronym, write it out in full for yourself. If you are confident you know something, don't bother rewriting it for the 100th time. After all, these notes are just for your own learning process.

Personally, I benefited a lot from writing down as much as I needed to understand difficult concepts. Concepts I had a harder time wrapping my head around would take up more space and time, but I would never simply skip a topic because it was too difficult. There are tremendous resources out there for IB students, so when you don't understand something, don't hesitate to look up a YouTube video, consult a peer or a teacher or even simply re-read your textbook. Do make sure your notebook has the entire syllabus in it, because it will be worth gold to you when final exams roll around.

By staying consistent with your notes and studying an adequate amount for any unit tests or internal examinations, you will be inserting the new-found knowledge into your long-term memory. You'll be surprised how much of a difference this makes when the final exam comes around! It alleviates the need of cramming the night before the exam, and instead trains you to understand the material, allowing you to apply it in different situations. And isn't that what the IB is all about: being able to apply knowledge to unknown situations?

Time Management

Having me preach to you about the importance of time management is perhaps hypocrisy at its best. For me it was not until I got into university that I really started to understand how effective time management can be. If you are one of the few who has mastered the skill at an early age, then consider yourself lucky. This is an invaluable ability that you will use regularly throughout your life.

One of the great rewards of undertaking the IB challenge is that you will have the opportunity to learn amazing time-management skills. The key to good time management is not just writing up a good schedule, but also imposing consequences when you fail to adhere to that schedule.

For example, if you promised to revise biology for 45 minutes a day every weekday and then you only manage to do 15 minutes on one of days, you must make sure you catch up on the remaining half an hour the day after.

Pro Tip: an extremely helpful Reddit thread on revision tips can be found here:

https://www.reddit.com/r/IBO/comments/7yg8uj/resources_studying_tips/

When Do I Start?

I had a teacher who once told the class (with 4 months remaining until final exams), "I hope your revision is going well… and if there are still some of you that haven't started revising, well you are already behind."

Hearing those words, I got uncomfortably nervous and stressed. Not only had I not begun revising, but I also didn't even know where to start. Several weeks passed as I procrastinated even more and eventually "mock exams" came around. I didn't study much, except for glancing over a few past papers from the previous year.

Luckily, it turned out that some of the "mock exams" were in fact last year's actual examinations. Nonetheless, I didn't have a good feeling about the whole thing and my grades reflected this – I got a 36 overall with a 4 in HL Mathematics. This was a real wakeup call as my university offer was given on the condition that I get a minimum of 40 points overall and a 7 in HL Mathematics and Economics. I feared the worst.

With less than a month to revise and no quick solution in sight, I was probably justified in my distress. Some of my friends had been "revising" since the beginning of winter break. I was too busy partying and procrastinating. With less than a month to go until exams I knew that this month would make or break me.

I quickly made a demanding exam schedule and started it the following day. For a whole month I practically lived in a cave, having deactivated Facebook and deleted WhatsApp. I read, breathed and lived revision. The only thing that kept me going was a voice in the back of my head telling me "you did nothing for two years, the least you can do is work mercilessly for one month, and then it will be all over."

The whole point of that little story is not to suggest that you should only leave a month for revision. It was simply to demonstrate to you what you will have to go through *if you do* leave revision so late. I was never one to miss a party – there was no way I could give up weekends, and sports, and all my hobbies just so that I could start revision many months in advance. I left the revision too late, and I paid the price. Whatever choice you make, you need to realize that you will have to bear the consequences when your actual exam preparation comes around.

There is no ideal time to start revising. That being said, you should never leave less than a month, and you would probably be wasting your time starting revision any sooner than 5 months before exams. Personally, I would recommend starting around one and a half months before the final exams.

Some of you may seem confused as to why I am suggesting that you don't study too much, but that's not what I am saying. There have been studies done that show how students can reach the "peak" of their revision too early and have a "meltdown" before actual exams. This usually happens to students that start revising nearly a year in advance. By revising too much in advance you may run the risk of failing to recall the earliest information and start to panic.

Perhaps the golden rule to IB exam revision can be worked out logically. If you still have assignments to finish that will be graded by the IB, it's probably safe to say that you should not even think about starting revising.

Your Internal Assessment is far more important than early revision so make sure you get that out the way first. Once all your work has been sent off you can drop everything else and just focus on revising for your exams.

Always remember your priorities: first get all the IA out of the way, and then you can center all your attention on revision.

The IB is too demanding for you to be starting revision early. With all the tests, assignments, sports meetings, CAS reports and homework that you will have on your hands, you will not be able to begin preparing too much in advance.

> **Pro Tip:** avoid burnout by planning your revision wisely. If you start too early, there is a chance you could get overwhelmed

Don't forget, however, that all the tests and coursework that you are doing is a form of revision. It's not the best, but at least you are doing something to reinforce your knowledge of the subject. So, don't think you are doomed if you haven't been revising out of a textbook with a month to go before exams. You have been revising "indirectly". At least that's what I told myself to be able to sleep at night.

Mock Examinations

Most schools will administer "mock" (or practice) examinations several weeks or months prior to the actual exams. This is not really a test of your knowledge and how well you will perform on the actual exam. It's more to get you familiar with examination conduct and protocol. You will need to get used to arriving punctually, having the right materials, and following exam rules and regulations.

Nonetheless, as previously mentioned, I suggest you make full use of your mock exams and treat them almost as if they were the real deal. You will be able to see what you would achieve if you had sat the real exam and not done any revision. Thus, it is kind of a test of how focused you were in class throughout the year. For most of you this experience will be a wake-up call.

Once your mock exam results come out don't just glance at the grade and move forward. Find out where you went wrong and where you could have done better. Although these exams are graded by your teachers, it doesn't mean the marking will be much different when done by examiners elsewhere. Look for places where you lost marks due to silly mistakes and try to work on these mistakes before your real examination.

One final note on mock examinations. It is no hidden secret that most schools use last year's real paper as the current year's mock paper. Don't think that you are a genius for figuring this out. This has been a tradition in most schools, however some now started to come up with new material. So don't actively go searching for this past paper and doing it; this defeats the purpose of the mock exams!

Nonetheless, if your mock exam paper happens to be a past paper that you have already worked on yourself then don't feel guilty or feel like you didn't deserve the grade you got. If you did well that just shows that your work with past papers has been worthwhile. You were able to apply the material again, meaning you probably learnt something along the way. If you still did poorly despite having seen the paper and the markscheme beforehand then you have reason to worry.

Time Allocation

You should by now realize that you will not be devoting an equal share of revision time to each subject. Some subjects you may not even bother with until perhaps a few weeks before the final exam. Other subjects you may like to start revising several months in advance. This will all depend on what your strengths are, as well as what your aims are.

For example: my IB results needed to coincide with my university offer from Oxford – I didn't really care about much else. This meant that I needed a 40 overall, 7's in HL Mathematics and HL Economics, as well as 6's in all of my remaining subjects. As soon as I learnt of this offer, I immediately outlined my problem areas. I knew that getting a 7 in HL Mathematics was by far my greatest weakness.

I had never gotten a 7 in any test and was probably averaging out a 5 overall. I felt uncomfortable with a large portion of the material. I also knew that getting a minimum of 6 in HL Geography and SL English should not be too big of a problem. I felt very comfortable with the Geography material, and my IA for English seemed good enough. Having gone over all of this in my head, I began to formulate how I will go about revising. I ended up spending more than 50% of my revision on Mathematics (doing a past paper almost every other night), then 30% on Economics (because I couldn't take any risks as I had to get a 7) and the rest of time I divided equally amongst the remaining subjects.

> **Pro Tip:** in the run up to exams, try not to study too many subjects on any given day. In fact, it is often advised to devote a day or half-day to a certain subject. Mixing up too much doesn't let you focus. And really get into the groove of the material

This may come as a shock to a lot of you. How can one spend more than half of their revision time on just one subject? Instinctively, you would want to divide your time equally amongst the six subjects giving you an equal chance of doing well in all of them. This is not the correct way to think.

You need to identify your weaknesses and base your revision around this. If you are borderline failing Chemistry and sailing through Business Management, then focus all your attention on getting through the Chemistry material. You may not enjoy it as much as BM but it's by far more important to you and your overall grade.

Figure out what your problem areas are by looking at your predicted grades and talking to your teachers to check where you stand in terms of their predictions. More importantly, you should know by now what your aims and objectives are.

Do you need a minimum of a 6 in this subject for university or university credits?

Do you need a 7 in this in order to fulfill the requirements?

Once you work out what you are aiming for then make sure to focus your energy on this specifically. If you don't have any set goals and you are just trying to get the greatest points total, then your task may be slightly easier. Find out where your Achilles heel lies and focus on this and this alone.

Another way you can look at it is the percentage of your grade that this paper takes up, and the amount of unknown content it requires. You want to start with those that give you the biggest output with the least effort. If two papers weight 30% but one is just biochemistry and another is, well, EVERYTHING else, cram the first one and then slowly switch to the second.

How Do I Revise?

Although there are a multitude of methods to revise for the actual exams, you need to be careful and avoid doing redundant tasks. Out of all the possible methods that are out there, I highly recommend you try to focus your revision around **past papers**. For a full detailed explanation of this method please refer to the specified chapter on Past Papers.

I know that this method may not work for everyone. Perhaps you made great notes throughout the year or you enjoy learning from the syllabus and the textbook. Nonetheless, more often than not the most successful IB candidates will tell you that they revised primarily with the help of past papers and markschemes.

If you still insist on studying from textbooks and notes, I recommend you cover some basic study tips. For example, some subjects such as biology may require more 'visual learner' skills – using your eyes and memory to recall the information. I know some students get very creative with this process and create highly effective 'mind maps' and 'word association' memory tools. I guess the theme here is sticking to the revision method that you know works for you the best. If you don't think you have one, I highly suggest you get cracking on past papers.

> **Pro Tip**: keep consulting your teachers – even in the weeks before exams when you may not have school. They are there to help you.

No matter what method you choose, I highly recommend that your revision remains active. By this I mean you are constantly writing, making notes, and writing again.

Although lying in the grass with a book to cover your face from the sun sounds like a good plan, you are wasting your time. Sit at a desk, grab some plain white paper, and make good use of your pen and pencil. You are twice as likely to remember what you are revising if you are constantly writing and not just reading.

> **Pro Tip:** be careful with writing notes as a 'revision' technique. This is like learning to swim by reading a book. You actually need to be doing questions and not just reading stuff and regurgitating it.

Despite the various study techniques out there, I still want to outline one study method which you can use as a framework to build your personalized, perfect study plan. This approach focuses heavily on the use of past-papers, and also relies on the fact that you have been taking adequate notes throughout the two years of IB.

1. Make Revision Sheets or Flashcards

Making flashcards is that typical study tool that most people have used at least once in their academic career. However, a lot of people also don't use them correctly: the learning happens from MAKING the flashcards, not from just aimlessly reading over someone else's. Personally, I prefer making revision sheets. They're pretty self-explanatory, after all, it's a REVISION sheet. To make these, go back into your notes (yes, the ones I told you were crucial), and using a nice fine-tip pen, start writing only the very **important** information on one sheet of A4 paper. Depending on the length of the unit, you might need to use both sides of the sheet, but very rarely should you use more than that. This way, it seems less daunting to learn all the material. Now, you might be wondering, how do I know what's important? Well, you can start by thinking back to old tests: which questions came up, and where in my notes do I find the answers to that?

In addition to this, your teacher might have mentioned specific questions that always show up on exams that are crucial to know. You can also look up notes for the class online and see what those people have included. Be wary though: this might not be everything you need to know! And lastly, you will just know how to follow your intuition. Trust me on that one.

Now, without having realized it, you will have re-learnt a whole unit by making a revision sheet (or flashcards). You will have gone through all your notes, looked at old tests and re-read up on concepts you hadn't fully grasped yet. All of the important things are on your revision sheet, which you can glance at the night before the exam or use to answer past-paper questions when you're stuck. Repeat this process with all your units (yes, ALL), and you will be all set on knowing your content for your exams. Don't underestimate the time this takes. Ideally, make a schedule, allocating enough time to each subject, with enough time to relax in between.

2. Past Papers!

The second step is to **apply** the knowledge by doing past papers. As is made clear in the chapter on past papers, in order to succeed in the IB, you must be doing past papers consistently. At first, you might want to be using your revision sheet to help you through the papers. For example, when outlining your first few history or economics essays, it might prove helpful to look over your notes so that you can start off strong. However, as you start to become more and more familiar with the content, try and do the past-papers under test-conditions: time limits and no extra notes. Only this way will you become an expert at doing exams. For a more in-detail overview of the use of past-papers, refer to the previous section.

3. Big posters

Another great method, especially for content-heavy subjects are posters. My technique is: solve a full past paper, grade yourself with markschemes as harshly as you can, find your weakest points. Restudy the material and write the correct answer down on an A2 paper dedicated to this topic (e.g. biochemistry, kinetics, human physiology). You will notice that you know some topics already well-enough and some took you 4 posters to study in full. Hang them around your room and look through them during small breaks. If you make the same mistake again - rewrite it, but change how you formulate it, or add a diagram or at least color code it. Repeat it orally a few times. This method is great especially for biology, as you can see the links between topics that would've been on different pages in your notebook.

4. Prepare your essays and examples together

This one we used for literature p2 and economics p1. The point is that there is a limited amount of things they can ask you, and it's easy enough to prepare the answers in advance. Collect your real-world examples, put down each interesting point you've found on these two texts you chose. Usually, it's more productive to do this as a group, and then each picks the ones they find the easiest to remember and apply in the essay. Prepare quotes, statistics, and during revision just systemize them in a way that makes it easy to look through before exams. These skeletons that you made can be then adapted for different related questions, and it allows you not to panic when the exam starts.

5. Quizzing each other

If you want to make sure that you'll get that 7, there is one step that comes after doing all the past papers from your parents' birth year. It's also effective revision a day before exams, but it's more of a revision of revision thing. Ingredients: classmate (1), syllabus guide or a good study guide (1), time and will to go until the end (the more the merrier). It's better to find someone you have different strengths and weaknesses with. So, you sit in the library or in zoom, and quiz each other on everything you think you might not know by heart. Another sits and checks your answers, adding things you've missed in the end or explaining fully the answer if you don't know it at all somehow. The point is that talking is faster than writing, and with another person waiting there's more pressure to know the answer and formulate it faster - like in the exam room.

Study Groups

Some of you may find that study groups work well for particular subjects. I myself found it extremely useful to work together on a math paper with another person, or to discuss economics material in a group. Choose your groups wisely though.

Avoid students who are far more advanced than you and avoid friends that seem like they attend revision sessions more for the social aspect rather than actual studying.

The point is that if you find revising or working through past papers with a group of equally motivated peers useful then by all means proceed with that.

> **Pro Tip:** make sure to choose study friends wisely! Some kids will only stress you out, and others will slow down your revision...

Online Study Groups

With the rise in popularity of the forums and social media tools we discussed in our Internet chapter, it is no surprise that there are now dozens of ways for you to form study groups with IB kids around the world.

Do give this a try and see if it works for you – some of the study groups are very effective. However, if it is clearly not helping you learn, then be sure to leave the group and go back to a more established revision method.

Being Productive

You will probably have a good week or two of no school before your examinations begin so make full use of that period. Make sure each day is productive and that you set yourself mental tasks to complete every day. Don't be alarmed but you should probably be aiming to get at least 7 hours of pure revision done every day that week. This isn't really asking that much given that you probably haven't been doing much revision all year.

Don't panic if you come across something during your revision that you have never seen before. Chances are it probably isn't in the syllabus anymore or maybe you just missed it out in class. Ask your friends or your teacher for advice. You shouldn't spend hours and hours stuck on one section or problem – remember this should be revision and not first-time learning.

Another common mistake made during the revision period is setting yourself goals that are simply beyond your reach. No one expects you to revise for twelve hours a day straight, sleep for eight and leave four hours for washing/pooping /eating. It shouldn't have to come to that. You should be studying hard but also leaving a little time to relax and recover. Remember that there is a huge amount of resources available for you to aid in your revision.

Pro Tip: many students swear by the app Anki – it is meant to really help with remembering things easily. For a full guide on using Anki for your memorization-based subjects, please check out: https://www.reddit.com/r/IBO/wiki/usefulapps

---

Cramming: The Night Before

No words of advice or comfort can really help ease your pre-exam stress and make you relax the night before your first examination. You will remember that date for a long time. For most of you, this is probably the first official externally graded examination that you take (unless you've done GCSEs or SATs). This can be a scary thought, but you just need to realize that in a matter of a few weeks all of this will be over, and you will embark on the longest holiday of your teenage life.

Now, what should you be doing the night before an exam? Well, as a golden rule, you should restrict your revising only to material that will be examined the following day. This means if you have a math exam tomorrow, you should be doing just math today – not biology which you have in a week's time or something like that. You need to keep the subject fresh and familiar in your mind – focus all your energy on it the night before and hopefully you will wake up with most of it still in your head.

Now, what about cramming? There is a heated debate as to whether cramming even works. Some say that having late night cram sessions is not only ineffective, but that it can put you in unnecessary stress and increase your chances of "going blank" the following day.

Others will tell you that cramming is the best form of revision, and everything you stuff into your brain the night before just spills on your exam paper the next morning.

Then there are also those who will tell you that cramming works – but you should not do it because you are not learning long-term, you are merely memorizing stuff in the short-term which you will probably forget in a weeks' time. Those people are missing the point.

From a personal viewpoint, cramming the night before an IB examination was helpful, but only to a certain extent (and only for certain subjects). For example, I found that cramming popular mathematical proofs was extremely helpful, however cramming an English novel was not.

Use your common sense a little when it comes to cramming. More importantly, don't overdo it. Your sleep and nutrition can play a large role in your examinations, so make sure you are getting a minimum of six hours of sleep most of the days.

Exceptions can be made when you have an exam the following day, and then after that you have a day or two-day break from exams for recovery – in that scenario I have seen some students even pull off near all-nighters.

I really don't recommend that though- sleep is more valuable than you'd think!

Disappointment: The Morning After

However well your exam went, you are more than likely to come out feeling rather disappointed. This is natural. If you come out of the exam room very cheery and happy that usually means that either you have been very lucky and really aced it, or you really messed up a question or two because you misunderstood what was being asked.

Either way, the most important thing to remember after every examination is to move on. Don't hang around outside the exam halls asking all your friends what they answered or what they thought of a certain question. The exam is over. Whatever you say or do after is not going to change what you wrote on that paper or the outcome of the exam. You need to revise for your other papers.

This is one of the biggest mistakes I see students make when it comes to revision. Instead of studying for the next paper, they waste time talking to their friends and trying to figure out how they got this or that answer, or what they wrote about in their essay.

> **Pro Tip:** avoid going online and asking people how they thought the exam went and what answers they got. Most forums implement a 48hr rule where you can't discuss the exam and, more importantly, you will not solve anything by discussing the past.

You are likely to get even more disappointed and discouraged if you waste time asking your friends what they wrote down only to find out that your answer was totally different. After you have just sat an examination, just go home as fast as you can and focus on the next one.

Moreover, if you have finished the last paper for a certain subject, then make sure you get that subject totally out of your head. Clear all the notes and papers for that subject out of the way and pretend that you don't even know what it is. Instead of doing six subjects, you are now only doing five. It is of vital importance that you make the transition from one subject to the next as smooth as you can as the exam schedules can be very hectic.

Method of Elimination: A Technique

One factor that separates the more successful exam candidates from the others is that they have picked up certain examination techniques along the way. One of these is a revision technique by which you use a process of elimination to make an educated guess as to what might show up on the next paper. Let me give you an example: when I sat my HL Economics exam, Paper 1 had a big question on monopolies, but neither Paper 1 nor 2 had anything on negative externalities. I made an educated guess that there would be a big question on negative externalities on the Paper 3, with little emphasis on monopolies. This was indeed the case that year.

You can do this for almost any paper. Each subject has its key syllabus areas on which students should be examined. This is perhaps truer for Group 3, 4 and 5 subjects than the others. You can use the process of elimination to make a clever guess as to what could potentially show up on the next paper having already sat the first one. Discuss this with your friends as they probably have a similar inkling. This technique, combined with cramming, can practically make you an overnight expert on an area with which you were previously not that comfortable.

Last Minute Revision

You need to make full use of the last few moments before you enter the examination room. Find a nice quiet place to quickly run through key points and get any last-minute cramming done. Avoid large groups of people as you will probably not be able to concentrate that well.

You should probably even revise in the car/bus ride to the examination place. Just don't waste any valuable time that you have on useless distractions.

Don't Panic

As cliché as it sounds, probably the most important thing to remember in those weeks/months before your first exam is to NOT STRESS. I know it's easier said than done, but when you panic, you retain less information, and you sleep worse, and it's not good for your mental health.

It's perfectly normal to feel stressed. We all do. For some of us (most of us I would imagine) it can determine your future. Yes, if you fail them you can probably be creative and salvage, but that doesn't mean that the university you end up in is insignificant. However, try to enjoy yourself as much as you can. Try to ignore the stress as much as you can and see the fun in the revision and the exams. I know it sounds really weird, but if you can find redeeming features about the work you have to do, you can do more of it and you will suffer less.

Make sure to avoid panic-inducing situations and people. Remember that you got this, you can do it!

Study Drugs

Some students in the IB have claimed to take study drugs such as Ritalin and Modafinil (Adderall) in order to enhance their performance, however these cases are very rare and usually it is a doctor's prescription for ADHD.

Also, multiple studies have been done in universities showing that people who use them have lower GPAs than people who don't use them. he high concentration levels and hours glued to the screen without breaks from the drug does kind of make you wear out after taking them

My two cents: it wouldn't be worth the risk doing it as an approach and if they create negative effects it could completely mess up your performance. Stick to caffeine, water and lots of sleep!

Final Thoughts

Your IB exam scores do not determine your worth, value to society, or success in the future.

It's natural to feel this stressed during exams but I wanted to remind you that who you are as a person is not determined by the2 numbers you'll see in July.

Put forth an effort that reflects your character and aim for the top. But know that in 5 years, you won't be remembered by the specific scores you earn. A 45 won't be nearly as impressive to the real world as it is in the world of IB.

You may be remembered by your intelligence, but your kindness, perseverance, dignity, and honor will form lasting impressions.

I've tutored IB for about 10 years and love this program and the opportunities it creates, but I also think it's important to separate identity and performance.

Though I don't know you, I'm proud of the journeys you've taken to get to this place. Only you know the challenges you've faced, yet you've persevered and can see the finish line. Don't stop running here, but don't ignore the entire race if you stumble at the end.

CHAPTER 13

HOW TO TAKE EXAMS LIKE A BOSS

'IB? More like I be screwed with all these exams.'

Although you should keep in mind that you need specific revision techniques for each individual subject, there remains much to be said about examination techniques in general.

Your success in the exams will not only rely on how well prepared you are in terms of the material, but also how well you perform under pressure. To deal with this you will need to master a few exam techniques. Most of them are simple, but nonetheless are often forgotten or severely underestimated.

Time Management

You need to be able to allocate your time proportionally across the entire duration of the exam. This includes taking off a few minutes from the beginning for reading and the end for proofreading. Whatever time you devote to actual writing and working out should be spaced out across the whole exam.

Luckily, the IB have made your task even simpler as they now indicate how many points each question and sub-question is worth. For most papers this is the same year in year out however pay close attention to this as it will decide how many minutes you will need to spend on the question. If it takes you less time to answer than you had anticipated, then move on to the next question as you may need that extra time.

You absolutely must not, and under no exceptions, hand in your exam without having attempted all the questions from beginning to end. If you have not answered all the questions that were required of you then you can consider your grade 7 a missed opportunity.

> **Pro Tip:** improve your time management by treating your past paper revision as if it was the real thing

Once the examiner sees that you have left questions at the end blank, this immediately sends out a signal that you have mismanaged your time. This mistake is made every year by countless bright students and the only reason for it is poor organization and time use – something that is not expected from the best candidates.

There is absolutely no reason why you should not have enough time to finish the exam. I hear this excuse all the time, but the truth is you did have enough time, you just didn't use it wisely. It's one thing to leave a question blank because you just had no idea how to answer it – which is something I also highly discourage. But it's a totally different matter if you didn't answer the last few questions because you messed up your timing.

Treat every piece of work (that is assessed for IB purposes) as if it were key, because in a sense it is. You can't really afford to have an examination component be a 4 or a 5 if you want to get a 7. Mathematically it might be possible to score just right everywhere else and get a 6 or a 7 but you are only making your life harder. If you treat every piece of work as critical, you'll have a consistent set of work which then gives you the flexibility that if you make a mistake due to stress or whatever, it won't ruin you.

Command Terms

These 'command terms' are specific words and phrases that the IB like to use in their exam questions. The IB examiners are not just trying to grade you on your knowledge of the subject, but they want to test your ability to answer the question that they have set out for you.

This is not something that is unique to the IB examinations. At university, and also in some job applications, you will be tested on your ability to really understand what is being asked. There is no point in answering how something happened if the question asked why it happened. Get used to reading questions carefully and answering accordingly because this is a skill that you will reuse often.

> **Pro Tip:** build your own list of command terms – writing them down and explaining them will reinforce your understanding of them

Again, your success at identifying and answering these command terms will largely depend on your practice with past papers. That being said, no amount of preparation can spare you from being careless. For this reason, make sure to double-check what is being asked.

If time is available, then I even recommend you highlight or underline the command term so that you don't forget what it is you need to answer. There's nothing worse than writing an answer explaining something when you were simply asked to define it.

A full list and explanation of command terms can be found in the syllabus/subject guide for the subject in question. These can be found online, or by asking your teacher. The terms differ from subject to subject. Please make sure you understand the command terms well before you go into the exams.

Extra Materials

There are very strict rules on what you can bring into the exam room: a clear bottle, pens, a ruler, a pencil and an eraser are all allowed. I highly recommend you bring all of these (without the ruler for language exams). In previous years, wristwatches were allowed, but that is no longer true due to the increasing prevalence of smart watches. However, don't be alarmed, your teachers are responsible for having large clocks in the exam rooms so you are always aware of the time. They will also announce certain time intervals, such as 30 minutes left or 5 minutes to go.

I always have a little bit of paranoia when it comes to calculators malfunctioning in exams, so I strongly recommend that you bring a spare calculator (not necessarily the graphing one) or at least replace the batteries the week before the exam. It goes without saying that you need a spare pen or two just in case the one you have runs out. Also, try to bring a set of highlighters because you can use these to remind yourself of the key terms in a question as discussed before in this chapter.

Students often also forget that you can ask for extra paper. If you are struggling with a long math or physics problem, and just need extra paper to try some different approaches, just ask! The same goes for needing extra space to outline a psychology and economics essay before starting the question. It will often result in better, and more coherent, answers to longer questions. If you are solving a math problem on scrap paper, do remember to re-write the essential steps on your actual answer booklet (or on the exam paper), as there are worth several important marks! If you've noticed that you can never fill everything into the box in your past papers and mocks - ask for extra paper during reading time. Worst case scenario - you won't use it. Usually, the teacher asks who may need some, so just raise your hand and continue reading.

In some subjects you'll have paper 1 and 3 at the same time with a break in between. While you won't be allowed to access any technology at this time, you can bring your notes, posters and flashcards to go through them. Use this time to refocus, do some last-minute short memory revision and ace this second paper. Don't discuss the previous paper - you can always do this afterwards, but now you have more points to conquer.

Answer the Whole Question + Nothing but the Question

This is self-explanatory. When answering any question on the IB exams you must make sure you address the exact phrasing in the question and give the examiner exactly what he/she is looking for. For all my examinations, I brought along a highlighter or two so that I could highlight key words in the question sentence.

For example, if a math question stated "give the answer in cm3" I would highlight (or underline) the cm3 part. I know that this might sound a little pointless and a waste of time, but you would be surprised to see how many candidates "forget" certain parts of the question. One common example is when a question asks you to "explain why" and you write an excellent essay on "how". By highlighting the "explain why" part you will significantly reduce the chances of this kind of slip up.

> **Pro Tip**: don't feel upset or frustrated if the exam didn't test 90% of what you studied extensively – that's just the nature of these exams. Focus on that 10%, and then move on

There is usually absolutely no reason to write more than what is required. If the question is worth two marks this means the examiner is probably looking for two key points – no more, no less. You don't have time to write everything you know.

You need to pick the most valuable bits of information and keep to your own time limit. There are no "bonus" points and you will not get extra credit for writing what is not required. Remember, the key is to write efficiently and aim for maximum marks with minimum nonsense.

Less is More – Usually

There are a few exceptions to the above paragraphs. If, in the unlikely scenario that you stumble upon a question you don't know how to fully answer, then sometimes (very rarely!) writing something that you do know on the topic might give you a few marks.

This technique is very beneficial if used wisely, but it can also be very risky and damaging to your time if you abuse it. I can give you a good example.

Suppose you get a "define" question worth two marks. This usually means you need to give two concrete points in order to get full marks.

> **Pro Tip:** every question counts! We are talking about extremely fine margins here – imagine you fail your diploma by one point and that one point could have been achieved if you had just decided to answer that one question you skipped..

Let's suppose that you could only remember one. Whereas normally I would suggest that you not waste your time and just move on to the next question, there will be times when a little bit more 'filler' might get you that other mark. Either expand on your first point or throw in some other information that could, maybe, give you the remaining mark (like adding an example).

> **Pro Tip:** there is no clear consensus on whether this works. In fact, I would only recommend it if you already think you have secured a high mark on the paper. If you are struggling with every other question, then don't waste time and only answer correctly

Remember that you will not get marked down for writing more. Indirectly, you always run the risk of losing valuable time. There is a general belief that examiners will only read the first few points you make and ignore the rest if you haven't hit the nail on the head yet. Personally, I find that this notion is too general to apply to every examiner in every subject. Your best bet is to keep writing "educated guesses" until you think you have good odds at getting most of the marks. You won't lose marks, but you might not gain any either. Remember that you are facing a balancing act – writing more BS versus having more time to answer later questions.

Give Yourself Space

One of the first things you should do when you sit at your desk is carefully lay out all your materials. You don't want to be doing a three-hour examination curled up uncomfortably in a tiny working space.

Place the examination paper on one side and the fill-in answer booklet next to it. Arrange your pencil case and all of your materials somewhere neatly in the corner. Make sure that your workspace is not one giant mess or else this could reflect negatively on your answers.

I would place your water bottle (if you brought one), on the floor next to your desk. There would be nothing worse than your bottle leaking onto your exam paper!

Start with What You Know

If the exam is parts-based, then I highly advise you to start with the parts where you are more comfortable and ones that you find more enjoyable. Not only will this ensure that you do not waste time attempting trickier questions, but you will also feel more confident and optimistic knowing that you have already answered many questions correctly.

There is no strict rule governing where you need to start and finish your section-based exam so don't treat it in a strictly chronological order. Do what you feel happier doing first and leave the trickier bits for later.

For many papers I used a three-step strategy. So, you have 5 minutes of reading time - notice the questions you find the easiest and quickest. Then the ones that might take you longer. Start your exam with simple ones, circling or otherwise marking those you save for later. Then repeat, leaving only the hardcore no-idea ones. Finish up with writing everything you think might give you some points in the last ones. In the last 5-10 minutes, proofread, adding new points if you have time to.

Bonus: for huge exams like chemistry paper 2 you can make a checklist of all questions and cross out those you're done with. I don't recommend jumping to the next question without finishing the previous one as you will lose time on understanding the context when you come back.

Reading time

Abuse these 5 minutes. Bring the juice out of them. What you need to do is plan your exam: pick a question if there's a choice, mentally weigh the options, and understand the order that you will answer questions in. If you still have time left - begin mentally answering the question, bring up all the statistics you looked through 15 minutes ago, all the facts, steps. In your first few minutes after reading time, you need to put down everything you have in your short-term memory - there's a high chance you will forget the inflation number etc. These are 5 minutes of planning and focusing on what's important, don't lose them.

Handwriting

Do you have handwriting that needs its own Rosetta Stone? If so, you need to make at least some effort to improve it or else you risk having your paper deciphered angrily and possibly downgraded. I highly suggest that when you are doing past papers in your revision, you start to focus also on the neatness of your handwriting. I personally haven't heard of any cases where a student's paper was simply illegible, but I am sure that they exist.

> **Pro Tip:** if you have a legit medical condition or reason – you may request to use a computer/laptop. This does not include having chicken shit handwriting!

If you find that your writing speed is significantly slower, then you might be better off not bothering with drastically improving your handwriting. If your teachers need to constantly remind you to write neater then please do pay attention. Nothing is more frustrating to an examiner than to decode your cluttered calligraphy.

Leaving Early

There are very few things in the world that frustrate and anger me more than seeing candidates get up and leave examinations with plenty of time to spare. You are given the time limit for a reason – use it! You must be incredibly careless to give up and just leave the exam with an hour to spare. There is absolutely no reason – none whatsoever – for you to leave before the time is up.

> **Pro Tip:** if you really have an abundance of time left – try to go over every question as pretend you are the examiner. Have you squeezed out every mark possible?

Don't think you can just cross your arms on your desk and put your head down for a nap either. That would be equally stupid. I don't care whether you think you have answered all the questions and proofread enough. Unless you are 100% confident that you got 100% don't even consider leaving early. And no, you're not "cool" or "rebellious" for leaving with time to spare.

Proofreading

You absolutely must make sure you leave a few minutes at the end of your examination for proofreading. This is more important in non-essay-based exams such as Mathematics and the Group 4 topics. Even in examinations for Economics, going back and making sure your diagrams are properly labeled could score you a few extra points. I'm not suggesting you make sure that you crossed all your T's and dotted all of your I's but at least make sure the majority of the exam is legible and that you avoided any silly mistakes.

The few marks that you pick up when proofreading could prove vital if you're on the edge between two distinct marks. You will lose and gain most of your marks at the beginning and at the end of your examination – so make sure you make a positive start and always go back and proofread at the end.

Ignoring Distractions

Although the exams are supposed to happen in complete silence there may be times when distractions are simply inevitable. For example, the kid sitting next to you who has never heard of cough medicine and is having non-stop bronchitis-like coughing. Or the student who accidentally drops his pencil only for it to roll all the way across the room.

I remember for one of my first Mathematics exams the weather in the morning was terrible. It was hailing, raining and thundering all at once. The fact that our examination center had a semi-glass ceiling provided a very surreal Dolby-Digital surround sound. It was probably the most frustrating thing to encounter when you are trying to focus on an HL Mathematics paper.

You need to teach yourself how to work around distractions. Don't become frustrated and punch the desk. Nor should you start to complain and lash out on your examination coordinator for having so many distractions.

Just sit your exam and focus on what's in front of you. Do whatever you need to do to clear your head and relax. If you know that it's an issue for you - practice in advance. Study with your siblings screaming around. Study in a coffee shop without headphones. I even studied in the IB office, where everybody was talking all the time and you had to learn to ignore it.

Last Minute Exam Checklist

Have you done the following before entering your exam:

- Did you bring two pencils and two pens? (and colored pencils – if you do geography, or a ruler - if you do economics...)

- Are they sharpened / refilled?

- Is your calculator charged?

- Do you have at least 1 L of water for every 2 hours the exam goes on?

It may seem obvious, but when I did the exams, I forgot some of these due to stress, and thus did not score as highly as I could have scored.

Trust me, you'll want to have water when you're staring down at a 20-mark multi-part physics question. The point is to spare yourself the misery and just make sure you've prepared your stationery and water beforehand. However, don't drink so much water that you have to take a bathroom break and waste valuable exam time – this is a mistake that too many students also make.

How to prepare mentally

Exams can be scary, but let's face it - IBs aren't your first or last ones. Something that helped me is developing an exam state of mind before during the SATs and APs. You can create artificial exams or use mocks for this too. My strategy was 9 hours of sleep, an espresso and no breakfast (if it's a morning session), however, yours might be different. The point is, learn what brings you to your most productive and abuse this state as much as you can. You can also create a some sort of ritual to put your brain in the exam mode.

Another tip is to use studying as escapism. This is stupid, but during my exams I was more worried about how much weight I put on due to stress than about actual results, however, this made me study harder because I tried to get away from these thoughts so hard that solving math for 7 hours was a relief. You can use your fear of exams to your advantage - just focus on the past paper you're doing and let it drive out all your anxiety.

Final Words of Motivation

You did it. You are literally in the final stretch now

You woke up every day. You went to school, and somehow you survived years of your life in those desks. You somewhat paid attention. You worked on your CAS. On your EE. On your IAs. The way, how, doesn't matter. You did work. You spent countless hours sitting in class, sitting back home, doing what you are supposed to do. You are over it. There is no going back.

Whichever way you did it, you are here. You have so many hours of invisible preparation that you never thought that it would count, but it does! That time you played Kahoot, and you actually discussed that question. You remember that. That time when someone made a joke about a funny science or historical name. You remember that. You most probably have notes. You look at them, and you know what's there. Or at least you remember - something.

There is no way of going in and not knowing anything.

You are a soldier. You volunteered to do this insane 2 years of this operation called IB, and here you are. You survived! How?! IT DOESN'T

MATTER. You did it champ. You have been trained by every homework, every reflection, every classwork, every presentation, every paper, every word that daily has reached your ears - to be ready now.

No, you are not 100% prepared. None of us are. If someone says so, well let me tell you: they are not. We have no idea what's in the papers. But the best we can do is to trust ourselves. You got up every day, you suffered, probably you cried, you fought so much already. There is no way you are giving it up right now.

Look at yourself. Where were you 2 years ago? Did you know anything about your subjects? Now just take a deep breath and think. Yes. There is something in your mind about everything.

Revise. Keep that knowledge fresh but be kind to yourself.

Hope this helps! Good luck guys!

CHAPTER 14

HOW TO COMPLETE CAS

'does this count for CAS?'

This chapter will be kept very short. If you are honestly struggling with CAS then I cannot do much for you except shake my head in disappointment.

The good thing about CAS is that it gets everyone involved in the community, teaches students to be creative and aims to keep everyone in good health. The sad thing is: if you were really that concerned with community service, wouldn't you be doing it already, instead of being "rewarded" for it with CAS? However, that is not our concern. Your aim is to get your project and finish it as soon as you can (preferably while still in your first IB year) with minimal difficulty.

Creativity, activity, service (CAS) is one of the three essential elements that every student must complete as part of the Diploma Programme.

Studied throughout the Diploma Programme, CAS involves students in a range of activities alongside their academic studies.

It is not formally assessed. However, students reflect on their CAS experiences as part of the DP and provide evidence of achieving the seven learning outcomes for CAS.

In order to demonstrate these concepts, students are required to undertake a CAS Project. The project challenges students to:

- show initiative
- demonstrate perseverance
- develop skills such as collaboration, problem solving and decision making.

How is CAS structured?

The three strands of CAS, which are often interwoven with particular activities, are characterized as follows:

Creativity – arts, and other experiences that involve creative thinking.

This is probably the 2nd easiest CAS component to fulfill. You don't need to be a young Mozart or Picasso to get your creativity activities. First and foremost, engage in school-based creativity activities. This includes any play productions, choirs, and art competitions. If that doesn't work out for you, do something independent for the school community. Design their website, make a new banner/poster to boost school spirit, teach younger students how to draw/Photoshop/act.

Activity – physical exertion contributing to a healthy lifestyle, complementing academic work elsewhere in the DP.

This should be very straightforward. I know what it's like to be lazy and non-athletic more than anyone else, but even I managed to get my hours with absolute ease. I joined the school sports teams not only for the sportive factor but also simply because it was a lot of fun. If you go through high school never having tried out for the football, basketball, swimming, volleyball, tennis or even track and field teams then you are missing out on a lot of memorable experiences.

Even the non-athletic kids at my school somehow found their way to the local gym and at least lifted some weights or did some treadmill running. There is always some solution available. It could even be as simple as trying to walk 10,000 steps each day.

Service – an unpaid and voluntary exchange that has a learning benefit for the student. The rights, dignity and autonomy of all those involved are respected.

This is the problem area for most people. I don't think it's because we are all inherently selfish and egotistical, but it is perhaps more to do with a problem in finding service work. If your CAS coordinator (assuming your school has a CAS coordinator) is living up to the expectations, then you should be able to get advice and opportunities via him/her. I know schools treat CAS and especially the service component in varying degrees of seriousness. Nonetheless, you need to ensure you did enough to make the IB moderator satisfied with your CAS reflections.

The type of service you do will largely depend on where you live, how comfortable you are being outdoors, how fluent you are in the domestic language, and a variety of other factors that would make it too difficult to give you any specific tasks. Like I said before, no one is asking you to create a charity overnight or clean oil spills and create peace in the Middle East. You just need to demonstrate that you care enough about the community.

What is the significance of CAS?

According to the IBO, CAS enables students to enhance their personal and interpersonal development by learning through experience. It provides opportunities for self-determination and collaboration with others, fostering a sense of accomplishment and enjoyment from their work. At the same time, CAS is an important counterbalance to the academic pressures of the DP.

CAS varies a lot from school to school. I only had to have thirty reflections, so I did a couple of weekly things and reflected on them whenever anything interesting happened. Ideally you should do your CAS project in year one, so you have less to worry about during year two.

CAS Coordinator

As aforementioned, the school's CAS coordinator will largely decide the success of your school's CAS program. When I did the IB, the CAS coordinator was wonderful. Not only did he make sure that everyone did what was required of them, he also made sure that those who tried to cheat the system were sufficiently punished. Your CAS coordinator will either be very engaging and hunt you down if you are slacking (for your own good of course) or he will be easy-going and let you decide what you want to do and when you want to do it. The latter approach is a bit too risky for my liking.

> **Pro Tip:** be nice to your CAS coordinator. There's a good chance they are doing this job voluntarily and it's actually not that easy.

At the end of the day, you just have to make the best of what you've got. If your CAS coordinator doesn't seem to care about whether you pass or not, then that just means you will have to work that little bit extra than the student who has a CAS coordinator who does everything for him. Having a poorly run CAS program is not a good enough reason for failing to meet the CAS component requirements.

Tips

Although my CAS advice lacks much detail, I can offer you a few words of advice on the CAS program in general.

Completion – make sure you complete the CAS program as early as possible. I'm not saying you give up on all creative, athletic and community-related aspects of your life for the remainder of your IB experience, however it will be more beneficial for you to complete CAS as soon as possible. I was done with most of the CAS requirements before I stepped into IBY2. This did require a lot of work to be done while I was in 11th grade (including many weekends working, and also a school trip to help paint/build a school in Morocco during Autumn break).

> **Pro Tip:** Get CAS done as soon as possible, or at least do the minimum requirements. The more work you get out of the way, the better. You'll thank yourself in IB year 2 for getting CAS done early

My IB coordinator offered the opportunity to begin CAS work as early as 10th grade (a year before IB began). Those who seized this opportunity were rewarded because they would have the entire last year of their IB without the CAS burden on their shoulders. I had friends who were being chased down for a good part of grade 12 and this stress reflected on their other IB work.

The lesson here is that the sooner you finish CAS, the sooner you can start to worry about all the other work you have to juggle for the IB. Get this out of the way as soon as you can – even if that means working in hospitals and running marathons every weekend in your first few months of IB.

Writing your Reflections – make sure you keep a very clean and tidy track record of all your CAS activities. For some activities, you will be required to write up an evaluation. Do this as soon as you finish the work, otherwise you will just forget what you did. Keep in mind that reflections can come in many forms, and most CAS coordinators will be accepting of you submitting video reflections as well! Keep all this information in a very safe place and don't lose it because there will be a day when your CAS coordinator will ask for it.

Faking It – just don't do it. How damn hard is it to legitimately do the work? If you think you can forge your tennis coach's signature, then don't act too surprised when your CAS coordinator calls him up only to find out you never did the 10 hours of tennis lessons that you claimed. There's nothing sneakier and more self-centered than claiming you helped your community when really all you did was just cheat. You will probably get caught and feel guilty as you are made an example of in front of your friends. Just do the hours – it's not that much to ask.

While on the subject of misconduct, please avoid asking for CAS recognition when you know you didn't deserve it. This includes doing paid work, tasks for your family, favors for your friends, and any other clever ideas you might have to score some easy CAS points. Don't end up like this. Not only do you risk being caught, you're also better off just doing real CAS work and benefiting from the experience.

University

One massive advantage that you will have over other non-IB university applicants (and even job applicants) is that you can use your CAS experience to build up your CV/application. Community service looks great when applying to competitive universities, as do creative abilities and an athletic lifestyle. Make the most use of your CAS program at school because it will be of great use in later life. Even in my current CV I still have elements of community service that I did during CAS.

For this very reason, I strongly suggest that you make full use of your CAS program and do service activities that are more attractive than others. For example, organizing a concert at the retirement home is a lot more eye-catching on your CV than handing out pamphlets or walking dogs. In fact, any service work that requires engagement with people you would not normally work with is very impressive to universities and employers.

For this reason, you should ensure to do CAS service activities that actually mean something. Similarly, playing for the school football team is more effective than spending an hour a day at the gym because it shows that you can cooperate with others and work in a team. Choose activities that you might want to impress with later on in life.

Failure

If you fail your entire IB Diploma because you did not meet the CAS requirements then there is little hope for you. I have seen some of the worst IB candidates still manage to scrape through their CAS so for you this certainly should not be a problem. Don't overestimate CAS as it really should not dominate your IB schedule. Then again, don't leave it as the last thing on your to-do list because it will harm your other IB work.

A lot of students dread CAS. I don't understand this. CAS allows you to have a positive impact on your community. I promise you that if you are dedicated and actually spend time once or twice a week on an activity that helps others around you, you will feel so much better. People that simply study all the time can never get the best grades because they eventually burn out and feel too much stress. So, it's important you actually do things you like or have interests in.

You should treat CAS as that much needed oxygen that's saving you from drowning. Try to pursue activities that you are genuinely interested in and don't just volunteer so that you can submit some arbitrary number of hours to your advisor. Give value to the world, and you will be paid back handsomely in the long-term.

I know for a fact that playing football for the school team had a huge benefit on my life in the IB. After those practice sessions I felt better, my mood was elevated, and it's always nice to be away from books once in a while. What I'm trying to say is that CAS is actually a really, really good aspect of the IB. It turns us into more open-minded individuals and gives us time to pursue our passions.

#TrashTag Challenge – A simple solution

A few years ago, there was a viral internet challenge that was making the rounds. And this time it wasn't something stupid like kicking a bottle cap or dousing yourself with an ice bucket.

I'm talking about the #TrashTag challenge

It's not often that a viral hashtag on social media goes, well, beyond social media. But this online challenge encouraging users to clean up places has seen tens of thousands of people doing just that.

In the TrashTag Challenge, users pick a place filled with litter, clean it up, and post before and after pictures. Volunteers have made beaches, parks and roads trash-free while also raising awareness of the quantity of plastic litter we produce.

Capitalizing on that viral momentum, I set up an Instagram account called @CASglobalprojects and encouraged students to submit their photos there with the following rallying cry:

> "GUYS I JUST HAD AN IDEA FOR A GLOBAL CAS INITIATIVE! can we make this a thing please?! like how cool would it be if it was IB kids around the world that made this go viral? Talk to your CAS coordinators.. and we need a trendy hashtag.. #Trash4CAS? ##IBtrashkids #IBtrashChallenge #CAStrashchallenge ? "

To my surprise, the page took off and is now followed by over 1000 kids at hundreds of IB different schools around the world. Here is an example of one of the posts:

Thus, if you are struggling to come up with any CAS project ideas, I **highly suggest** you implement a similar program at your school. I will be more than happy to share your before and after photos on the IG page. Be sure to use the #Trash4CAS hashtag and encourage others to get involved.

Why do I like this concept so much? Without getting too preachy, I do think we have f*cked our planet in so many ways, so we need to take on environmental initiatives. You want to keep your local neighborhood and community clean. This is such a cool way to do that. Also, if you argue correctly, it counts as a hybrid activity as it entails both service and activity.

Warning: If you decide to take on this challenge, please wear proper gloves and be careful around things like needles! A trash-grabber is also a good idea.

Managebac

As for reporting your CAS reflections, I hope your school uses Managebac. If it doesn't, talk to your coordinator and make them consider getting it for the school. It really makes the process a lot easier (even though Managebac has its own headaches).

Final Thoughts

Remember, CAS is either a pass or a fail. CAS doesn't affect your number score, but if you don't complete the requirements you won't get your diploma (and this DOES happen occasionally). So, make sure that's not you, because that would be the stupidest way to fail to get your Diploma.

There is even a rumor of a student who got 40+ but failed because he didn't meet the CAS requirement... make sure that's not you!

CHAPTER 15
HOW TO GET ALL 3 BONUS POINTS

"The bonus points are like those 3 mushrooms you get at the start of Mario Kart – somehow everyone keeps wasting them'

So, before you dive into the mysterious world of IB additional points you may want to ask yourself: "Who am I to listen to some stranger's advice on what to do for my TOK and EE?"

What I can offer you is fool-proof advice and techniques on how to get A's in both your TOK and EE without having to work your butt off too much.

If you follow my advice correctly and put in some effort and determination, you can, I firmly believe, obtain a grade A in both. If, however, you are someone less ambitious and are just struggling to get the grade in one of the components, then just flip to the relevant section. And, finally, if you are someone who is predicted to fail your EE and doesn't have a clue about how to pass TOK, then this chapter is definitely also for you.

The IB "bonus point" system is a gift to you. They are basically asking you whether you want three more points to be added to your final total. Why would you say no? I have seen some of the smartest and hardest-working students fail to achieve all three.

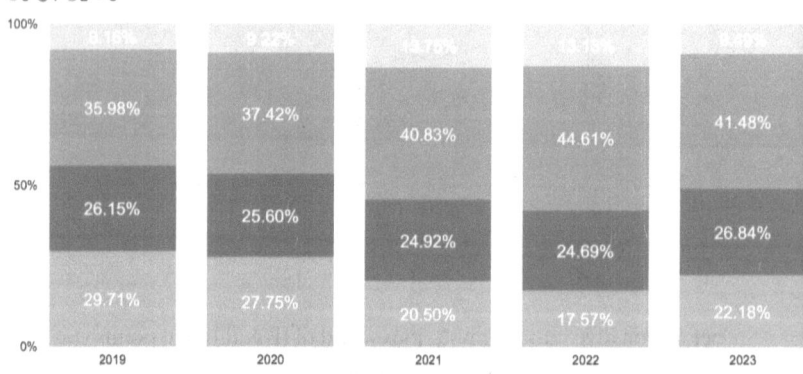

source: https://www.ibo.org/globalassets/new-structure/about-the-ib/pdfs/dp-cp-provisional-statistical-bulletin-may-2023.pdf

As you can see, every year (except 2021-22, due to covid), fewer than 10% achieve all 3 bonus points. So why is this?

All you need to do is get one A and one B in either your EE or TOK. So, if you aim for As in both, then surely you will get an A in at least one of them, right?

Well, I only wish it was that easy. The bad news is that you need to work extremely hard to achieve a grade A in either of the two components. The good news is that anyone, of any academic ability, no matter how clever, can achieve the three points.

You need to get your priorities straight – if you know that you can afford to miss out on those three points because all you need is a pass and you're predicted about 35, then focus on getting a point, maybe two. However, if you are barely passing, and are in desperate need to squeeze some points out anywhere you can find – the "additional points" are the perfect place to start.

You need to get it through your head that these are not bonus points. No matter what you call it – bonus, additional, core, or extra points – your final score isn't given out of 42, it's out of 45.

In fact, in recent years the IB has tried to remind students that the Diploma is a complete package and the points are part of the total score. Therefore, you need to do all that you can to make sure you get all three.

The Extended Essay

Let's take a look at some M23 statistics again:

DP Extended Essay

% Grade Distribution by Subject Group

Result	Grade awarded						No grade awarded		Total
Group	A	B	C	D	E	Total	N	Total	
Studies in Language and Literature	15.2%	26.6%	37.5%	18.9%	1.0%	**99.3%**	0.7%	**0.7%**	100.0%
Language acquisition	16.8%	24.6%	40.0%	17.6%	0.5%	**99.5%**	0.5%	**0.5%**	100.0%
Individuals and societies	7.2%	21.3%	41.5%	27.5%	1.8%	**99.2%**	0.8%	**0.8%**	100.0%
Sciences	7.9%	30.5%	44.4%	15.6%	0.9%	**99.4%**	0.6%	**0.6%**	100.0%
Mathematics	8.8%	26.5%	44.3%	19.3%	0.4%	**99.3%**	0.7%	**0.7%**	100.0%
The arts	14.2%	21.3%	35.3%	25.4%	3.0%	**99.1%**	0.9%	**0.9%**	100.0%
Interdisciplinary	9.3%	26.4%	46.2%	16.4%	1.0%	**99.2%**	0.8%	**0.8%**	100.0%
Total	**10.1%**	**24.4%**	**40.8%**	**22.5%**	**1.4%**	**99.3%**	**0.7%**	**0.7%**	**100.0%**

source: https://www.ibo.org/globalassets/new-structure/about-the-ib/pdfs/dp-cp-provisional-statistical-bulletin-may-2023.pdf

As you can infer from the data, very few people (10.1%) get an A on their EE. This varies from subject to subject. For example, in Language Acquisition there are significantly more A's (16.8%) than in the worst group – Individuals and Societies (which has less than 7.2% getting an A).

Studies in Language and Literature and Language acquisition also have a fairly decent number of students achieving a grade A (15.2%).

Let's see if we can infer more from data about individual subject popularity:

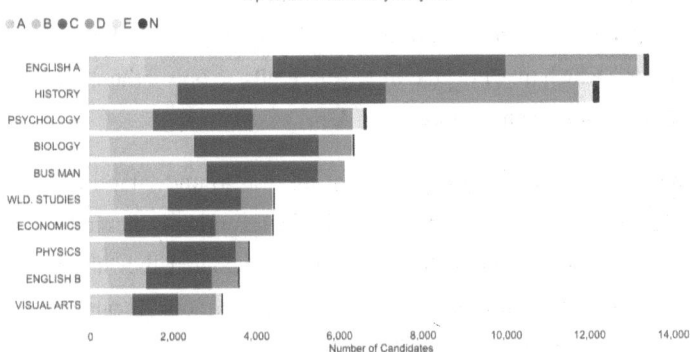

source: https://www.ibo.org/globalassets/new-structure/about-the-ib/pdfs/dp-cp-provisional-statistical-bulletin-may-2023.pdf

Unsurprisingly, History and English essays make up the bulk of subjects chosen. Mathematics had so few EEs (2250) that it did not even make the graph. There was also a surprisingly little number of visual arts EE's – despite getting the highest percentage of As.

Of the many people who choose to do a History or English EE - a worrying amount get a grade C or D. I would urge aspiring Historians to take this into account, as well as anyone who thinks an English EE is the "easiest".

You should not be overly intimidated by the EE – but you do need to take it very seriously. The sooner you begin working on it, the better.

Another important thing is that EEs are often easier to predict your grade on than TOK. Your conceptual, philosophical thinking can be very subjective, and though you might have put a lot of effort into your TOK essay and exhibition, there's still a big enough chance that the examiner just won't like it enough to give you an A or even B. On the other hand, EE is a research paper - a format that you can find infinite good and bad examples of. You know when the question you pick is deep enough, when the methodology gives you a precise enough answer, when you've evaluated many opinions and sources. The point is that TOK is a bit of a wildcard, which may not guarantee you results, so one of the strategies is to polish your EE and ensure it's an A.

The hardest part of an EE, at least for me, was to understand what this thing is. I started many times, changed subjects and only picked the final question in September of DP2. Honestly, don't do that, the only reason I still succeeded was my ultra understanding and impossibly calm (at least on the outside) supervisor, without him I'd probably fail my diploma. What you want to do is choose a subject (usually one of your HLs - the skills and academic background you have will help you to catch everything faster). Then you want to look up some research done in it. Try to find topics that you cannot waste time on understanding fully, and really understand the structure and the way of thinking behind this creation. Take notes on things like how they chose their methodology, the presentation of the question's scientific background etc. (I did a chemistry EE, but analogous structures usually exist in one subject area). The IB wants you to have this first experience in research, and to nail it you need to really understand how a good research paper is written.

Then you need to choose a topic. Here I have two pieces of advice. First, pick something you will not get bored of. Remember that with each question there are winning methodologies that may not be accessible to you. Don't choose something you're not sure you can get good data on. To make sure of that, look up papers on this or similar research questions. How did they collect their data? Were there obvious downsides? Maybe you have a way of eliminating some of them? How did they process it?

All this you have to be done with before the end of DP1. Ideally, you should already have the data or at least all the arrangements to get it during the summer. Yes, it sounds hypocritical, but you may not get as

DP Theory of Knowledge

lucky as me, and sometimes life just is against you. Be prepared for it.

As for writing - it's probably the smoothest part if you already knew what you were doing when collecting the data. All these articles you looked up with similar questions - save them for later. Methodology evaluation, comparing results, what to look up for your intro - analyze these papers and try to replicate the thinking behind them.

Bonus1: *if you're not doing this yet, what helped me is to find the articles that my first found papers cite as sources. Dig deeper into the hole of academic debate and mystery and see how opinions on this question were formed from the beginning.*

Bonus2: *MyBib was life-changing. Don't treat it just as a way to produce a well-cited bibliography, it's a place to hold all your sources in so that nothing goes lost or uncited.*

Theory of Knowledge

We now turn our attention to TOK, and again we are presented with some data from the M23 exams:

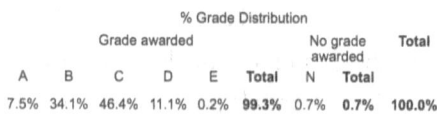

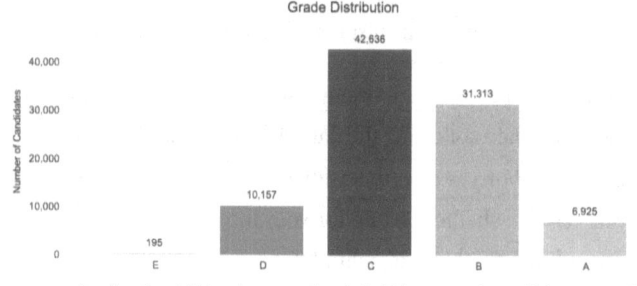

source: https://www.ibo.org/globalassets/new-structure/about-the-ib/pdfs/dp-cp-provisional-statistical-bulletin-may-2023.pdf

It is indeed rather bewildering how fewer than 7% manage to achieve a grade A in their TOK presentation.

The vast majority of grades for TOK are grade C

This, coupled with the EE data, shows a strong need for students to realize that they are giving up 1-2 bonus points every year.

For an in-depth 100-page guide on how to write your EE and complete your TOK, please consult my other guidebook: *Three: The Ultimate Student's Guide to Acing the Extended Essay and Theory of Knowledge*

CHAPTER 16
HOW TO CHEAT

'"Those who cheat on tests, I'm sure, will have their souls burned with sulfuric acid" – my IB Coordinator

I'm sorry. This chapter title is intentionally misleading.

There will be no actual cheating endorsed here.

But now that I've got your attention (and I hope this isn't the first chapter that you flicked through to), let's talk about academic dishonesty.

Remember that '1 out of 4 students fail' statistic we talked about at the beginning of the book? Well, a significant chunk of those kids failed their IB Diploma precisely because they thought they could be dishonest and get away with cheating:

"Failing conditions" for the diploma -- Scoring an "E" on your TOK or Extended Essay. Also not completing CAS. Note that this only applies to the diploma and not to individual courses. *The same is true for the academic malpractice (plagiarism) issue: it will affect that one course, but not any of your others. Obviously, that person would be ineligible for a diploma as well.*

The information I have provided so far in this book is in a way tricking the system without actually cheating. So, you are technically not doing anything wrong, you are just abusing certain aspects in order to get a higher grade – something that any clever student would do naturally.

This chapter won't give you the best tips on how to cheat. In fact, it will do quite the opposite – it will tell you why most methods of cheating fail and what the consequences usually mean.

You have to be pretty stupid to follow a two-year program only to then have your diploma taken away for academic malpractice. That's two years of your life practically wasted.

If you fail the IB diploma because of cheating, then you are pretty much screwed. Why risk two whole years of demanding work so that you can bump your grade up a little bit?

The risk is simply not worth the reward. It's even more redundant given that you can easily get a higher grade by simply following the guidelines set out in this book. No matter who you are, there is absolutely no reason for you to even think about cheating.

Although the IB originated in Switzerland, don't expect them to be very understanding, or "neutral" with regards to cheating. Any form of academic dishonesty is dealt with the utmost seriousness. The vast majority of the time when you are caught and reported you will lose your diploma. Not only does cheating carry serious risks but you will also put yourself under more pressure. The threat of being caught will make you underperform and provide an unnecessary distraction

Plagiarism

Plagiarism is probably the most common type of academic dishonesty found in the IB program. I'm not going to go into an in-depth discussion of what constitutes plagiarism and how to cite – your school should have already shoved that down your throat. I merely want to explain to you what happens when you try to do it. Hopefully this way you will avoid "accidentally" doing it and think twice before you complete any piece of work for the IB.

Many of you may have heard of the website turnitin.com. This website scans for plagiarism. Depending on what school you are in, you may have it that your teachers scan every single piece of work that you hand in electronically. For those of you that have no idea what I'm talking about let me explain: Turnitin.com (amongst many other more sophisticated websites) scans documents for any evidence of plagiarism. They take your words and check them across a multitude of various sources: websites, paid websites, written books, magazines, journals, etc. The program then composes a very in-depth report that specifies exactly how much of your document is plagiarized and to what degree.

These expensive plagiarism scanners that the IB use are growing in sophistication every year. Almost every possible essay-writing database is now listed, along with written books that have been made into eBooks. Even if you paid ridiculous money for someone to custom write your

Extended Essay, chances are the scanners at turnitin.com will catch it because they can afford to scan almost every database.

So, what does all of this mean for you? This should be a wakeup call for those of you who are likely to plagiarize "unintentionally." I'm talking about those of you who thought it was ok to throw in a few sentences here and there from your textbook because it's not available online. Almost everything is now available online and turnitin.com will scan these archives.

The consequences of plagiarism will more than likely lead to you failing that specific piece of work, and, depending on the degree of plagiarism, maybe even your entire diploma. I trust that you realize the dishonest aspect of plagiarism and will refrain from trying. More importantly however, I want to warn you to make sure that you don't accidentally and unintentionally plagiarize either.

I know that sentence doesn't make much sense, but it's for your own good that you make sure that none of your work is anyone else's words. So please, think twice before you include any sentence or idea that is clearly not your own.

WARNING: Never Share Your Work with Anyone

I feel obligated to tell you to never, ever, share your academic work online with strangers. Do not send it to anyone to read or verify or mark or give you feedback. Do not upload it on any plagiarism checking websites. Lastly, do not share it with your classmates unless you absolutely trust them.

Exam Cheating

Why in the world would you even contemplate cheating on the actual IB exam day? If you're at a respectable and honest IB school, then chances are that your exam center is going to have some of the most vigilant proctors making sure that your every breath and sneeze is natural. You and your fellow candidates are going to be like little sheep surrounded by a pack of wolves.

Even before you walk into the exam room your face will tell the whole story. Even the bravest of you that lack any conscience will struggle to conceal that nervous and tense look when you step into the room. Chances are that even before you actually begin to cheat, you will get caught cheating. This paragraph (and probably chapter) only applies to a small proportion of candidates out there, but nonetheless it's important to get the message out there that cheating on the exams is nearly impossible – and stupid.

Almost anything you can think of has already been taken into account. Random pre-exam calculator checks, plastic see-through bags, no talking in the exam center, assisted toilet breaks, only bottled water. For every cheating method there is already an answer. The only "cheating" left for you to do is to follow the legitimate advice and tips that I have been suggesting. On exam day the only thing you should be thinking of is the exam itself. Anything else on your mind will distract you from doing your best. The IB diploma is not some middle school exam where you can write the answers on the palm of your hand or slip in a cheat sheet. This is one of the most prestigious and respected high school programs in the world and they are not about to let their reputation slip as a result of academic malpractice.

As long as we are on the subject of cheating, there is one final word of warning. With the recent rise in cell phone and internet use, it has become almost inevitable that students discuss exam questions and answers online and over the phone. Make sure you are not amongst them. Schools have begun paying incredible attention to this and I have heard of cases where students were tracked through Instagram or WhatsApp and eventually stripped of their diploma because they broke several rules about revealing exam details before the examinations were completed worldwide.

> **Pro Tip:** be careful being in WhatsApp groups where students are asking for exam information. They will suspect that everyone in that group was part of the cheating

Given that the IB is an international program, there are small possibilities for the manipulation of time zones in order to get exam information. But again, let me warn you. Schools have begun to monitor students' cell phone use before and after the examinations. Also, more and more papers are being divided into several time zones. There's probably nothing worse than being fully ready for an examination only to turn the paper over and realize you have crammed the last hour into questions that are not there.

Also, if you are ever asked for question details from a friend living in the far west then please ignore them. Why would you want to make the same exam easier for someone else when at the end of the day you are going to be judged and graded in a somewhat standardized way? You are competing against other IB schools so don't put yourself at a disadvantage.

> **Pro Tip:** make sure you abide by the 24hr rule – you may not discuss the contents of exams for 24hrs after the completion of the exam. This includes asking stuff like 'was it easy' or 'what do you think grade boundaries will be?'. You have been warned.

Whistleblowing

Whistleblowing is a term used when an individual raises a genuine concern about suspected malpractice or wrongdoing and/or the covering up of malpractice or wrongdoing. Whistleblowing is different from raising a grievance. The IB takes whistleblowing very seriously. This policy describes how whistleblowing is distinct from both complaints and employment disputes or grievances that an individual may have. It also explains how you can raise your concern with the IB under this policy and how the IB will handle this concern.

For more information, please consult:

https://www.ibo.org/contentassets/fab8ccef45b743c0a68de6f9ea989385/ib-whistleblowing-policy-en-2018-1.pdf

Concluding Thoughts

The message here is pretty crystal clear: don't even try to cheat during your IB program because you will more than likely get caught and there is very little benefit. You can achieve amazing results without needing to plagiarize or be dishonest. Cheating will have severe repercussions for you later on in life. You can forget about going to any respectable university if your diploma is taken away because of academic dishonesty.

Not only is it a burden on your academic future but it also has serious social and familial consequences.

CHAPTER 17

HOW TO OPTIMIZE IBY1

'The first year of IB is the hardest...
if you don't count the second year'

Practice "skill" papers

After some time in IB you might notice that there are some more skill-based papers and some - more content-based. For instance, your Language A paper 1 will be an analysis of a random text that you've never covered, while your Chemistry paper 2 is impossible to write without thorough knowledge of the material. More in-between is econ paper 1 as you must use a fraction of content for your essay, or the data-based questions in biology. The thing is that in DP1 you can't write most of the content-based papers, but you can already practice in-full the skill-based ones. This will give you an edge on many fronts - in this specific paper, in writing content-based papers and IAs that require this skill and simply in being slightly faster in the classroom to notice things. By writing more and more practice skill-based papers you ease your life in DP2 as you will save a lot of time on both IAs and revision.

How to study for unit summatives

While you won't be able to write full papers until the end of syllabus for many subjects, acing unit summatives in DP1 is the best way to stay on top of your studies in DP2 (even if you don't have a great memory, it's easier and faster to revise than to study). They allow you to dive into each topic in depth, covering every little detail that might come up in your exam and probably will come up in your unit summative. Of course, the method below won't be the same for every subject and will require some adaptation, however, it will be useful for many. In the beginning it was developed for chemistry assessments. Requires about 3-4 hours depending on the amount of content, subject and how well you listened during lessons.

1. Go through all your notes or a textbook if you have a good one. Just read and try to notice the details and things you might be asked for. It shouldn't take over 30 minutes, ideally 10-15.
2. Open a previously prepared past papers per unit document (your teacher probably has one of those). Go through 20 questions, answering at first easy then harder ones. Try to do it as fast as you can, but it should take you no more than 30

minutes (e.g. for HL Chemistry paper 1 there are 60 minutes for 40 questions, hence why no more than half an hour). Check the markschemes. If you had 1-2 mistakes, restudy this part and move on to stage 3. If you had more, restudy the mistakes, maybe take some extra notes, and then try another 20 questions. *Bonus: while on the actual exam it's always better to put some answer than to not, while practicing try to mark the "not sure" questions too. There is no point in relying on luck in preparation, and if you had many "not sure" questions, then even if you got them right, there is a point in restudying the material, making some notes or maybe watching a few Youtube videos on the topic. This often puts you from a low to a high 7.*

3. Now turn to paper 2. I usually tried 2-4 chemistry questions at a time because they're quite long and there is no point in wasting so much time only to repeat the same mistakes. Then go through the mark scheme and grade yourself as harshly as you can, rob yourself from those precious points and highlight the mistakes. While doing that, take notes on your mistakes (e.g. "don't forget the units", "Analogous have different bone structure", or even a full algorithm for solving a type of questions if you really drowned in that one). Restudy what's missing, look again at fresh notes and take another round of questions. It should take you 2-3 rounds ideally, if you still don't comprehend you may need to ask your teacher or one of your classmates to explain it to you again.

4. The fourth step is more optional, but it's a great final brush to make in case you have time for that - take a mock summative.

Ask your teacher in advance to create one or make it yourself or find one. It should be timed, closed-book etc. Then check again, maybe a little less harsh, and ensure that you got a middle or high grade that you wanted. Else - find all the weak zones and restudy them, maybe take 2-3 similar questions.

5. Important - keep the notes you've made during preparation and read them thoroughly before the summative. You may also want to save them for DP2 exam revision. Of course, you will create new ones, but sometimes when we forget the concept there's no one better than our old self to explain the logic to us.

How to plan for IA and EE

This is something most people didn't do and wish they did. For me it was lack of understanding of the syllabus that stopped me, I felt like in DP2 I will know what I'm doing. The truth is that you rarely will, so you must go through this first-draft freeze as soon as possible.

Extended Essay

The thing with extended essay is that it will be way out of your syllabus, so actually knowing the whole syllabus will be of little help in most cases. If your essay is a science one, trust everybody around and at least collect the data in DP1. Most schools don't allow you to access the lab during summer, and you can't truly do anything aside from introduction without your data. There are so many things that can go wrong: you may not have the equipment, or maybe you have to order extra supplies, maybe you will lose all your data or somebody will throw your product away. Truly, don't risk it, there are things unfixable at the last minute. Logically, to have the data by the end of DP1 you need to pick a topic, research it, and find or create a methodology and actually understand why it's used. Also, it's good to keep in mind how you will analyze your data.

If you do that, you can write everything else during summer or (better) even earlier, but this is a base without which you're risking failure. For many other subjects there's some sort of data collection too, or at least an analogue of it. If you're interviewing people, there are always external risks, even if you're analyzing a book there will be a risk that you missed some huge detail. Your first draft will most likely be rubbish, and you need to have time to correct and rewrite it. Don't look at an extended essay as writing 4000 words, because you will probably rewrite 3000 of them. Leave time for that.

IAs

This, of course, is even more subject-specific, however, in terms of time management there are some common principles. Firstly, choose the topic, question, collect and analyze the data before the start of DP2. For some subjects that will be pretty much it (e.g. economics IA are 3 commentaries for an article - analysis of the data with some blended in evaluation). For others It will be just the beginning. I changed my biology data analysis three times, and that's a lot of work for one week but fairly little for two months. There are exceptions, for instance, if you want to have your IO based on books you will soon cover, you might want to wait and see what valuable details from your lessons you can add, however, it doesn't stop you from reading or rereading that book, finding articles, analysis videos on it, and creating some draft bullet points.

How to be ahead

Often we would spend most of our studying time preparing for summatives and exams, however, it turns out that the best students are those who pair it with preparation for lessons. It's not just about reading the textbook a few chapters in advance, though that can never hurt. It's about having some context around your knowledge, that you can apply the logic you learned in a broader sense than just your syllabus. This gives you an edge in that you start to think faster and understand instead of memorizing.

This context may come in different forms, and you can find whatever is suitable for you. Maybe you want to join a science club for chemistry experiments or listen to literature podcasts (even if they're not directly linked to the books you've covered, they still give you some ideas that may be paralleled or developed then in that last novel). There are an infinite number of Youtube videos from recorded university classes to just interesting channels that enhance your way of thinking for different subjects. You will have less time for that in DP2, but finding something that you enjoy and that tells you about the world outside of the syllabus guide is a great way to improve yourself and indirectly increase your grades.

Bonus: *making it a habit of some sort, or a way to enjoy learning outside of class enriches you as a person so much. For me long Youtube videos with a heavy amount of content were the main way of escapism in DP2, but it was made possible by the efforts to find what fascinates me outside of classroom in DP1.*

CHAPTER 18

HOW TO FIND THE PERFECT IB TUTOR

'Think about how bad the average IB teacher is... then realize that half of IB teachers are worse than that'

Ever since COVID showed us that online learning is possible and effective, there seems to be a huge boom in the number of IB students who now opt to have additional evening IB help – often using online tuition. This chapter will help you shed some light on whether you need a tutor, what you need a tutor for, and whether to take the traditional route of a face-to-face tutor or opt for someone online.

Do you need a tutor?

It should go without saying, but not *everyone* needs a tutor. When I was doing the IB, I was initially quite opposed to the idea (personal tutors were rare in my school) and my stubborn brain was thinking 'no, I am good enough at these subjects – no tutor is worth the money'. A few months before exams, I changed my mind (more on this in the following section).

The reality is that unfortunately not all teachers are good, whether they are new to the IB system, or just not a great teacher in general, so some students need tutors to actually explain and help students adapt to the curriculum. Some students want to learn ahead and cover more material when they are less busy in the beginning stages of the DP. Some students struggle with particular classes, and if a teacher cannot or is unwilling to give the extra lessons/attention required, then a tutor may be necessary

What do I need a tutor for?

Before you decide to hire a tutor, you need to know exactly what your aims and goals are. Allow me to share with you two anecdotes about my experience with IB tutors and how they completely changed the trajectory of my IB journey.

The first has to do with Language B, which for me was Dutch and I took it as an anticipated subject (completed the course in IBY1 and took the final exams in the first year so I would not have to do it in the 2nd year).

Although I was 'okay' at Dutch (my predicted mark was a 5 or 6), I was very worried about the oral exam component – which constituted almost 30% of the final mark. My Dutch teacher at the time was very strict with how much help she could provide us, and did not really wish to assist me in picking a topic or helping me plan the oral presentation.

It was at this point that the notion of hiring a tutor really first occurred to me. As I lived in Belgium, there was no shortage of Dutch tutors –

however it was very difficult to find one that knew what the IB was or had any experience with the qualification.

Nonetheless, I had a plan. I found this old sweet Belgian lady who worked as an English-Dutch tutor for over 30 years, and charged as little as 15 euro per hour. She had no idea what the IB was or what I would be examined on. Nonetheless, in the first session (I had 4 one hour sessions in total), I brough with me the grading criterion for the oral exam and told her *exactly* what I wanted to get out of the session. She listened carefully and made sure she fully understood the requirements.

She ended up suggesting a wonderfully topical and IB-rich subject for the oral (it was about integrating refugees in Belgium), and helped me plan my oral presentation accordingly, making sure I included as many idioms and Dutch phrases only an expert speaker would know.

The oral exam went perfectly. I was scored 27/30, and my exam was also selected for moderation which means they sent off the cassette tape with my oral to an external IB examiner. The moderated mark for the oral came back: 30/30. It was the best 60 euros I ever spent in my life. My teacher said it was the best oral exam she had ever witnessed in her 15 years of teaching Dutch B.

The second anecdote concerns Math HL. I received my offer from Oxford in early February of IBY2 and it said I had to get 40 points and all 7s at HL (which was Economics, Math, and Geography). As my predicted grade for Math HL was a 4, I was in deep shit. I knew I had to focus all my energy on Math or I would miss out on my dream university.

But even focusing on math and doing past papers did not help as much as I hoped. In the mock exams, I scored a low 5. It was at this point I realized I had to find a math tutor – and I had to find them fast.

As this was before the days of online tutoring, my options were very limited. I ended up finding a recent alumni from my school who was now doing a PhD in Mathematics at the University of Antwerp. He himself scored a high 7 in Math HL several years before. His rate was also very fair (25eur an hour) as he was a college student who just wanted to make some extra money.

I booked him for several sessions a week in the final months running up to exams, and he literally saved my Math grade. I ended up getting a 7 and the rest is history.

Beware of greed and exploitation

As the demand for IB tutoring skyrocketed in the last decade, so did the corporate greed of most IB tutoring companies. At the time of writing, nearly all of the 'top 10' of IB tutoring companies charge in excess of $100 per hour – of which they only pay 50% to their tutors and pocket the rest. This exploitation is not fair to the tutors nor the parents who are paying extraordinary rates for (what is often) mediocre quality tuition. It is no longer the case that tutoring companies hire the 'best of the best'. Now, most of the 'top 10' of IB tutoring companies let their A-level/AP teachers fill in the demand for IB tuition – this leads to very poor results.

Of course, it doesn't have to be like this. The internet allows you to search for tutors without paying silly rates to tutoring companies that pretend to act like matchmakers but really are just fancy middlemen profiting off the hard labor of their tutors (who are often forced to sign unfair contracts). You can use Reddit, Facebook, and Instagram to find freelance tutors for a fraction of the price.

RevisionDojo Tutoring

In the spring of 2023, RevisionDojo (who we discussed in chapter 7) launched an innovative platform to connect students/parents with IB tutors. The tuition is fixed at **$29 per hour** – with **100%** going directly to the tutor. No hidden greedy tutoring fees. No Bullshit.

I asked for several trial sessions with a handful of their tutors to gauge the quality and they were honestly as good (in most cases, better) than the best tutors from any of the 'big' IB tutoring companies. I was also given access to a database of 100+ tutors, all of whom had to undergo rigorous interviews and quality control before being listed on the website.

For these reasons, if you are looking for an IB tutor, we recommend using the RevisionDojo platform to find your perfect match. More details can be found at:

www.revisiondojo.com/tutoring

> **Pro Tip**: use promocode **SMARTBOOK20** to get 20% off Dojo+

CHAPTER 19

HOW TO REST AND RECOVER

'If there was a Sleeping HL module I would get a 7'

I warn you, I'm not an all-nighter kind of person. Efficiency is both about speed and result, and romanticizing lack of sleep, food and sacrificing everything for studying will hit you in the face at one random moment. However, the concept of efficiency applies to rest too, so in this chapter you will learn how to get rest without wasting your time.

Quality sleep.

Of course this varies from person to person, but overall, when we look at sleep we often talk about quantity. Everybody knows about the required 8 hours, not everybody gets them, especially IB students. What I found out is that you can feel rested by sleeping less if you pay more attention to your quality of sleep. Firstly, ensure that it's dark while you're asleep. This makes your sleep deeper and you feel more energized while sleeping less. Same applies to noise. Secondly, try to take a walk in the evening. Maybe go buy some groceries or return from a study session. At least open the window for ten minutes, and you will sleep better. Thirdly, try some sleep meditations or long Youtube videos with a sound that makes you fall asleep faster. Fourthly, there are herbs that help you deepen your sleep - lavender, motherwort etc. I actually used to rub lavender balm under my nose.

I often suffered from insomnia during the IB and found that I can't recall the material learned at these times despite being fully present during lessons. Therefore, months' worth of content had to be restudied before the exams and summatives, though technically I spent more time learning them. Lack of sleep affects your memory and ability to focus - the main things required for success in IB.

Quality food.

This one is something you've heard of; without proper nutrition there's no proper brain functioning. My way is simple - eat something that makes you feel better in the longer than 3 hours run. Ensure absence of blood sugar jumps so that you don't feel tired after eating. Research shows that adding fiber to and walking after your meals helps.

Bonus: skittles got me through DP2. Now it's not the best advice in terms of health, but if you need to write your IA for a couple more hours and you're falling asleep or if today's math lesson requires complete concentration, you can try to use it. You just eat one candy each time you're losing focus. If you're not in a constant sugar rush, this gives you enough energy to concentrate for about 10 minutes, so one pack can get you through it. Maybe it becomes more of a reflex at some point, but, you know, anything that helps.

Another thing is vitamins and minerals. If you have an opportunity to, test what's lacking and ask your doctor for some advice. Especially if you live in a northern climate, don't mistake your constant tiredness and malnutrition, maybe you're just iron deficient or something else.

Bonus: my immune system took a hit in the IB, I've never gotten sick this much in my entire life. The best thing IB teaches you is how to treat a cold in less than two days. My way - vitamin C, ginger tea with red pepper and extra spicy kimchi-jjigae. Works like a charm.

Work while resting, rest while working.

This is a mixed message here, but just stick with me. The diversity of tasks IB gives to you is insane, but it can actually be used to your advantage. Someone once told me that rest should be something opposite to your work. The way I apply it - there are work tasks and rest tasks, and they're totally subjective and can change over time. Maybe the precision of lab work actually calms you down, or you wanted to read and here's a book for English Literature. The most obvious example is CAS; it's not a work task to sit and draw for an hour if you do math most of the time, it's too different. There will always be more and less enjoyable parts of the IB, your goal is to separate them and create a mindset that the former are rest tasks.

With that said, I made two exceptions for that rule: socializing and overflow. While socializing can be incorporated in work, quality time with your loved ones or some in-the-moment memories should occur at least once a week. Drinking tea with your mom, going out with your best friends - these parts of life will let you stop and let go for several hours, which is an important part of rest. Overflow is a point where there is too much information and your brain just needs to process it. I found it helpful to lie in bed for 40 minutes after classes and before bed, just looking at the wall. Noticing my thought flow, it turned out that I was repeating and reliving my day. I quizzed myself on chemistry, made some points on what to add to my literature notes. It's hard to describe this state, but you're sort of in between sleep and wake when you just exist. Not really meditation from what I know, but that's where I really work. The hardest part is to learn how to remember all these ideas that you came up with, but even without it, it helped my revision enormously. Just make sure to set a timer, or you may sleep through something important, and your math teacher won't listen to your "I was solving those integrals in my sleep" story.

Find less time-consuming ways to become happier.

Eating your favorite pasta for dinner, hugging a friend, doodling during the break - find little joys in life and grasp them. You may not have the time for an hour-long walk, but you can take the longer route from the subway. If you learn to become ecstatic about a new pack of stickers you got (not to promote consumerism) or a teapot of jasmine tea, your life will become happier without much effort.

CHAPTER 19
HOW TO SURVIVE POST-IB
'I'm done.. what do I do with my life now?'

The day of your last exam will be a day that you remember for a very long time. I finished my last exam more than 10 years ago and I still remember that day as if it was yesterday. It will be a strange feeling. You go from having no free time at all, to suddenly having the longest and most carefree summer of your life. When you walk out of that exam room, you will want to celebrate but you will also be so incredibly exhausted that I suggest you go home and hibernate.

The reason I wanted to write a quick chapter on this is because I have seen over the years an alarming number of students suffer almost from a kind of post-IB depression. In the sense that they just don't know what to do with all this free time they have acquired. Students have even told me they feel like they don't have a purpose anymore, now that IB is finished. They feel empty inside and unsure about moving onto the next stage in life.

First off, know that what you're feeling is very normal. Even if your friends are not talking about it, there are tons of people reading this who feel much of what you feel. I felt it after most major milestones (high school, year by year in college, etc.). There are short-term and long-term things you should do, and I'll detail a few of them and why you should do them:

Exercise – even if you hate exercise, go take a walk. Go play tennis with a friend, or go swimming, or something. Do this at least 3-5 times per week, and you will soon find that you crave the activity. It will do wonders for your state of mind.

Get sunlight. It seems strange, but sunlight causes your body to release all sorts of things it needs, including neurotransmitters which regulate mood.

Read – you've spent the last two years reading mostly what others imposed on you, so you've built up some animosity toward reading. But you probably used to love it, and you can again (and it will make you healthier and happier). If you need suggestions, PM me.

Make others happy. Part of how we define our self-worth comes through service to others. So, go make someone's day. Maybe you take a younger sibling to some activity they love. Take your dog for a walk. Go volunteer somewhere not because you need CAS, but because helping people makes you feel better.

Long term, you have goals and a plan. What are the small steps you can take toward those goals now? Maybe you read a book or journal article for self-education. Maybe you work on a website. Maybe you browse the syllabi for the classes you're taking this fall and decide to start learning ahead of time?

Keep yourself busy and try to have some carefree fun.

WAITING FOR RESULTS DAY

My friend wrote this blog post for results day which I happen to find particularly poignant and incredibly well-written. With his permission, I have reprinted it here:

Today is not just another day. Everything you worked on for two years, all those sleepless nights and caffeine-powered mornings and awry lab experiments and tens of drafts of IAs and EEs and CAS reflections, all of these are being condensed into a two-digit number that might determine whether or not you're going to the college of your choice.

Today is the day.

You open Chrome, frantically typing the IB results website address on the search bar. Why is this taking forever to load?! You hurriedly key in your personal code and PIN and watch the page load faster than the speed of light. As you point the cursor at the 'Results' section, you think to yourself, "Shit." After an entire minute of thought, you click the 'Results' icon. The blue and white 1980s looking page finally loads and there lie your scores, gloriously glaring at you. What do you think they will be like?

Three things could happen:

You either got the results you wanted or got more than what you wanted.

You just missed your conditional offer.

You totally messed up.

If you got the results you wanted, congratulations! You just survived the world's most demanding, taxing, life-sucking curriculum. Go out with your friends, party, travel the world or stay at home and watch one more episode, because you can do that without feeling guilty.

On the other hand, if you just missed your conditional offer, the best thing for you to do is to express your feelings. Cry it out, or punch a pillow, or yell at yourself. Don't bottle up your feelings because you will end up hurting yourself, and at one point you will lash out on someone you really love. Accept what happened and learn from your mistakes. You could request the IB to remark your papers but if you're doing that, don't have any expectations because if your remarked grade is the same as your initial grade, you will undergo the entire "I'm-worth-nothing" phase. I want you to remember that no matter what, you did survive the IB. Yes, you relentlessly worked towards achieving your goal, but do you think you could've done something better? Do you think there's a reason you didn't get a 7 in ESS? Do you think there's a reason you didn't get a 6 in Math? If yes, improve.

Alternatively, if you missed your condition by a LOT, aka messed up, relax. If you want to retake your papers, that's totally fine but just remember that if you don't identify the reason you messed up in the first place, retaking the exams is pointless. If you're okay with that, go ahead but realistically speaking, not much would change.

Regardless of whether or not you fulfilled your conditional offer or met your expectations, ask yourself this – what is your definition of failure? Is it getting below a 24 in the IB or is it not living up to your expected or predicted grade? Either way, life isn't over. You failed. So what? The IB is just a small steppingstone of life but guess what? Life is filled with failure. At some point or another, you will fail. I guarantee that. And if not in the IB, you will fail elsewhere. You might fail your first exam in college, or you might fail to sell a product to a company, or you might fail to live up to your own expectations. The point is, there are two ways to look at failure: (i) either you keep cribbing about it, or (ii) you deal with it. You could keep saying, "Oh damn, dude, I failed. I don't deserve this. Why does life keep doing this to me? What have I done wrong? Why does this keep happening? God, can't you just leave me alone for once?!" Is this going to make a difference? Does cribbing change the fact that you failed? Does it mean you will never fail again? No, no, and no. Here's the thing: you're bound to fail in life. In fact, you should fail. Experienced and successful people have had their fair share of failure, but the difference between them and you is their mindset. They chose the second method – they chose to deal with failure while you chose to crib about it. They learn from their failures. You crib about it. They think of how they can do better the next time. You cried that you failed this time. They identify areas for improvement. You crib because you think you're doing your best. They accept the fact that they have failed and move on. You latch on to your failure and crib about it.

Today is not just another day.

You got your results. You're either happy or sad. But you know why today is not just another day? It's not because all your two years of hard work has been condensed into a two-digit number, no. It's because you chose to deal with your failure. You're going to move out of your home within two months. You're starting a new chapter of your life. This is the chapter that will greatly influence who you become in the future. So why not start off by accepting and learning from your failures? Because "if you learn from defeat, you haven't really lost"...

RESULTS

This section will guide you through your IB results: when your results will be released, how to access them, and how to request re-marks.

This information is based on a very helpful document circulated by the Facebook group: IB Students Worldwide, so I would like to thank them and credit them.

Logging on

On http://candidates.ibo.org you will be asked to log on with your personal code and PIN. Your personal code is composed of three letters followed by three numbers, and your PIN is composed of 8 characters. If you do not have this information, contact your coordinator. Note that the website may crash during the exact time your results are released, as too many students worldwide are also trying to access their results at the same time. You may get the message "Internal server error (500)" when trying to log on. This is usually resolved an hour later.

Once you are logged on, click on the "Results" tab on the top. The "Information" box near the top of this page should tell you about the exact time at which you can access your results. This time depends on the time zone of your school; it should be sometime between 12:00 to 16:00 GMT on July 6 (May session) / 13:00 to 18:00 in your school's time zone on

January 3 (Nov session). Note that every IB student in your school's time zone is assigned the same time.

Scroll down a bit on the Results page and you will see your results. You will find the grade out of 7 for each subject that you took in the session, along with your EE and TOK grades. At the bottom you will find your total points out of 45, along with an indicator of whether you have been awarded your Diploma. If you took two Language A subjects then it is a "Bilingual Diploma".

Example Timeline from May 2019

Date and time		Event
May session	Nov session	
July 5 12:00 GMT	January 3 07:00 to 12:00 in your school's time zone	Your coordinators receive your results first. Whether they are to share the results with you early is up to them. You can also start requesting enquiry upon results (re-marks and such) starting from this date. Universities also receive your results on this day (only if you had used IB's service that automatically sends out your results to various university institutions of your choice).
July 6 12:00 to 16:00 GMT*	January 3 13:00 to 18:00 in your	You receive your results on http://candidates.ibo.org.

	school's time zone*	*May students: You receive your results sometime between 12:00 to 16:00 GMT on this day. The "Results" tab on <u>the website</u> indicates the exact time at which you can access your results; it varies by your school's time zone. *Nov students: You receive your results sometime between 13:00 to 18:00 on this day in **your school's timezone**. You receive them exactly 6 hours after your coordinators receive them. The "Results" tab on <u>the website</u> indicates the exact time at which you can access your results; it varies by your school's timezone.
July 7 **12:00 GMT**	**January 4** **12:00 GMT**	Subject component grades (i.e. your marks on individual papers) are released to your coordinators. Whether they are to share them with you is up to them.
July 9 **12:00 GMT**	**January 6** **12:00 GMT**	Global results statistics and school results statistics are released to your coordinators. Whether they are to share these statistics with you is up to them.
August 31	**February 25**	IB releases this exam session's past papers for sale on the <u>Follet IB Store</u>. The entire pack costs $180 USD. It typically takes around 20 to 40 days for them to be leaked.
September/ October	**N/A**	May session only: IB releases the official grade boundaries sometime during September/October. IB does not release grade boundaries for the Nov session.
September 15	**March 15**	This is the last day on which you can request **enquiry upon results**. This refers to re-marks,

		requesting your scripts back, etc. These requests must be made through your coordinator.

Detailed Results

Clicking on "Detailed results" on the rightmost column of the Results page will yield the detailed results.

The detailed results show you the percentage mark you got for a subject, along with the grade boundaries for the grade you received as a result.

Use this information to determine whether you want to request a re-mark.

At this point, this is all the information that you will be given. Subject component grades (i.e. your marks on individual papers) are not given on this website; this information is sent to your coordinators from the IB the day after your results are released.

Results certificate

Your results will forever be saved on http://candidates.ibo.org; however, you may also keep them officially on record via a physical copy of your IB Diploma certificate. This certificate is a physical certificate that recognizes that you have passed the IB and received your IB Diploma (note: the "Diploma" *is* the certificate). On the certificate your grades for each subject are visible. Your school is responsible for sending you a physical or electronic copy of your IB Diploma certificate. It may take one or two months after you receive your results. An electronic copy of the certificate may be used for University applications. Note that the IB does, however, already have a service that automatically sends your results to various University institutions.

Component grades

On July 7 (May session) / January 4 (Nov session) at 12:00 GMT your coordinators will receive your subject component grades. Whether your coordinators are to share these component grades with you is up to them. Note that they do not consider re-marks.

The following image is one format in which your coordinator may download your component grades and send them to you.

Subject Details				
Grade	Raw mark	Moderated mark	Scaled mark	Subject
			88	MAY 2018 - MATHEMATICS SL in ENGLISH
6	16	16	16	EXPLORATION
7		82	36.44449	PAPER ONE
7		80	35.5556	PAPER TWO
			17	MAY 2018 - THEORY KNOWL. TK in ENGLISH
B	7	7	7	PRESENTATION WORK
C		5	10	THEORY OF KNOWLEDGE

All your subjects, including TOK and EE, will be shown; the above image shows the component grades of two subjects just as an example.

The first column, "Grade" shows the grade out of 7 you received for each component. The second column, "Raw mark" refers to the mark of your IAs and other internally assessed material prior to moderation. The moderated mark is then reflected in the third column - this is the final mark you receive for that component. If your work had not been selected for moderation, then it stays the same.

This third column is also the mark you received for externally assessed components. The candidate in this image, for instance, received an 82 for their Paper 1 in Math SL. The 82 is out of 90 marks; this is not shown here, and you would need to do your own research to find out the maximum mark for each component. The scaled mark is the mark relative to your entire subject, based on the weightings of each component. The weightings are also not shown here and must be deduced from your own research.

WHAT DO I DO IF I F*CKED UP?

Once you receive your examination results one of three things will happen. You may get the grades you were expecting and get what was required for your university. In this ideal scenario your IB adventure is over, and you can finally move on. Alternatively, you may receive your results and find out that you deservedly fell short in a subject or two, or perhaps failed something, and as a result your first-choice university offer is no longer an option. The final scenario is that you receive your results and find that there are a few subjects where you know you should have done better. You are shocked because, as things stand, you cannot get into your first-choice university or perhaps even your backup choice. There are several options that you may choose to take, outlined below:

Appealing

I'll be honest with you. When I first got my IB results in June, I did not get into my first university of choice. I got 42 points but fell short in HL

Mathematics because I got a 6 instead of the required 7. My offer from Oxford was 40+ points overall, with 7's in HL Mathematics and HL Economics. I wasn't too surprised because I knew if there was one subject where I might fall short, it was definitely math. Nonetheless, as things stood, I was not going to get a place at Oxford. I called up my coordinator and told him the situation. He highly recommended I appeal not just the mathematics grade, but also the 6's I got in SL English and SL Physics. The logic behind this was that if I didn't go up in math, then at least maybe Oxford would reconsider if I got 43 or 44 points overall.

After several weeks I was informed that my English and Physics grades would not improve. This was very disappointing because I felt that my English exams went perfectly, and I had superb IA marks for both English and Physics. I felt like there was no chance that my math grade would increase because first of all I was predicted a 5, and second of all because math is rather objective – there are right and wrong answers with little room for grey areas and errors by examiners . Well, I turned out to be mistaken. I received the news from my coordinator that the grade had gone up to a 7, so I had met my offer and got a total of 43 points.

The point of that little story is that you should not just try to appeal when you feel like you could have done better. Even in exams where you are 80% sure you cannot improve; it may be worthwhile appealing if your university choice is on the line. Of course, this will come at a financial cost, but I would say that if it is affecting your future then the financial cost is worth it. Besides, if the grade does change you will be refunded the full amount. Would I have appealed if I got my first choice of university and could see no direct benefits of a higher IB score? Probably not. I would recommend appealing only if it will affect your university decisions.

Enquiry Upon Results

Re-marks are a type of enquiry upon results (EUR). Such requests entail a fee and can be made only through your coordinator. The fee is paid by you to your school (unless your school is kind enough to pay it for you), who then forwards it to the IB. You have until September 15 (May session) / March 15 (Nov session) to make these requests. The table below is a good approximation of the fee structure. Note that your school may charge a higher fee to you due to labor work from their end.

Enquiry upon results	Fee (USD)		Time needed for request to be fulfilled after school submits request
	2015 version (page 157)	2017 version	
Category 1 (re-mark): A re-mark of externally assessed material for an individual candidate by subject. This does not include internally assessed material (e.g. IAs); refer to Category 3 for such.	$117	$120	Up to 18 days *On average: under 7 days*
Category 1 report (re-mark report): A report on a category 1 (re-mark) for an individual candidate. The report provides feedback and comments from the examiner who made the re-mark.	$201	$206	Up to 30 days
Category 2 (return of assessments): The return of externally assessed material by subject component to all candidates **(2A)** or an individual candidate by subject **(2B)**. For 2A your school can choose to receive this in either hard-copy or electronic format. For 2B it is	2A*: $85 2A^: $53 2B*: $18	2A: $54 2B: $18	2A*: Up to 20 days 2A^: Up to 10 days 2B^: Up to 10 days

electronic only. * refers to hard copy and ^ refers to electronic format.			
Category 3 (IA re-moderation): The re-moderation of internally assessments (IAs) by subject or level for all candidates.	$282	$289	Up to 40 days

Category 1 (re-mark)

Category 1 is the re-marking of externally assessed material for an individual candidate by subject. This does not include internally assessed material (e.g. IAs); refer to Category 3 for such. Take note of the following:

To request a re-mark, contact your coordinator.

Re-marks are made by subject. You can choose one or more subjects to re-mark.

The re-mark applies to all externally assessed components of a subject. External components refer to components that are marked by the IB examiners and not your school, i.e. Paper 1, 2, 3, etc. You can also re-mark your EE and TOK essay.

You cannot choose to re-mark only a particular component.

Internal components are not included in the re-mark. Internal components refer to your IAs as well as your TOK presentation. If you want your IAs re-moderated, refer to Category 3.

Re-marks do not apply to multiple-choice exam papers (Paper 1 of Phys/Bio/Chem/DT/SEHS).

You must pay a fee to your school for the re-mark. Your school is responsible for informing you of the fee; it is likely to be larger than what the IB requires in the table above, as your school may take in a portion of that fee for labor costs.

Your coordinator submits the re-mark request to the IB. It will take up to 18 days for the re-mark to complete, although it may take as low as a day (depending on the popularity of the subject). From previous sessions, most candidates had mentioned that it typically takes under 7 days for the majority of subjects.

The re-mark is usually completed by a different examiner to the one that originally marked your work. If you choose to re-mark a subject with very low candidate intake (e.g. Lithuanian A: Literature), the re-mark may be completed by the same examiner.

Your coordinator should contact you about updates to your re-mark.

Once the re-mark has been completed, your new grade will appear again on http://candidates.ibo.org.

This new grade will be higher, lower, or the same. Whatever this new grade is, it will replace your original grade. You cannot, for whatever reason, bring back the original grade.

The re-mark fee will be refunded entirely from the IB if the re-mark results in a change of grade, higher or lower. The grade refers of the subject grade out of 7, not your percentage mark. The IB returns the fee to your school; it is your school's responsibility to return the refund to you. You do not get a refund if there is no change of grade.

You cannot request a second re-mark for the same subject.

The IB has no limit on how many subjects you can request re-marks for.

You may also request and purchase a Category 1 report, which can again be done through your coordinator. The report provides details about the re-mark, including comments from the examiner who made the re-mark. Such a request must be made within a month of receiving the re-mark and will take up to 30 days to receive. Your coordinator will receive the report and forward it to you. It is generally not recommended to purchase a report, and not many students (or schools) decide to purchase one.

Category 2A and 2B (return of externally assessed work to school/candidate)

Under Category 2, the work by a student that is externally assessed is returned to the school or candidate, along with the comments made by the examiner(s) and the marks awarded. This may include exam papers, TOK, EE, coursework for art subjects, etc. Take note of the following:

Instructions to examiners state that comments are written on a candidate's work only if doing so is helpful to the examiner in the marking process. Therefore, if a candidate's work is returned, it may show only the marks allocated and may not include comments from the examiner.

A category 2 enquiry is for the purpose of returning assessment material only and does not constitute a candidate's claim of exclusive copyright in that material. If you want to claim exclusive copyright, a separate request must be sent to the Assessment Division, IB Global Center, Cardiff. This request should be made through your coordinator.

Category 2A is typically paid for by the school. It requests the work of all candidates in the cohort by subject component. For instance, your school may decide to purchase only the Paper 1s of a certain subject of all candidates in your cohort, for whatever reason. If you have knowledge that your school has purchased such, you may try contacting them if you would like your work back. It will take up to 20 days (hard copy)/10 days (electronic) for a Category 2A to be fulfilled, and your coordinator will be responsible for collecting them.

Category 2B is the return of externally assessed material by subject for an individual candidate. To request a Category 2B, contact your coordinator. Your coordinator will be responsible for receiving the work and sending it to you. Since it is by subject, you will receive all externally moderated components of that subject. Your coordinator will receive your work in electronic format (PDF) and will take up to 10 days.

Category 3 (re-moderation of IAs)

Category 3 refers to the re-moderation of IAs of a certain subject to all candidates in a cohort. This request is usually the decision of your school and not you as an individual candidate, since it affects all candidates in your cohort. If your school decides to make this request, it will take up to 40 days. This re-moderation can result in the same IA grade or increase in your IA grade. It will not result in a lowered IA grade. Unlike the Category 1 (re-mark), a change of grade does not result in a refund.

Retakes

If you have failed to receive your Diploma or are dissatisfied with your results, you can choose to re-take. Re-takes can be organized through your coordinator, who will then decide on the venue of the exam(s) that you plan to re-take.

In the unlikely scenario that you completely mess up your IB exams there is always the option of re-taking them in November. I am not a big fan of this option for several reasons. First of all, re-taking in the winter exam session still means that you will miss out on a year of university unless you can find somewhere that starts after the winter break. If not, you would be better off repeating the year and sitting the examinations in May

Second of all, re-taking exams is only a good option if you genuinely think that things will change. There is no point in redoing the exams if your approach is the same. If something tragic happened that distracted you from performing at your level, then retakes can be a good opportunity for a second chance. If, however, you failed to meet your targets because you did not prepare adequately, then chances are this will happen again during retakes.

For these reasons, retakes should only be considered as the final resort.

It goes without saying that if you missed a university offer by a small amount then you should first appeal your grades before you even consider retaking the exam.

CHAPTER 20

WTF IS AN IBDP? YOUR GUIDE TO IB ACRONYMS

'I only know of two acronyms now: IB and FML.'

Anticipated Student: students in the junior year of IB (11th grade) are sometimes referred to as "anticipated" students, in that they are anticipating completion of the IB DP in the following year. Likewise, any IB exams taken at the end of a student's junior year are called "anticipated exams" but still count toward completion of the Diploma. Students can take no more than 2 anticipated exams and only in SL courses.

ab initio: "From the Beginning: A Standard Level World Language Course. The ab initio language exam must be taken at the end of grade 12 and is equivalent to three language levels

Academic Misconduct: Any student action, intentional or unintentional, which leads to a student taking credit for another person's work or gaining any unfair advantage. This includes (but is not limited to) plagiarism, collusion, duplication of work, cheating in exams and falsifying a CAS record.

Anticipated Candidates: Junior students in the IB Diploma Programme

AP: Advanced Placement, an examination system run by the College Board which offers credit by examination for college courses. Some IB classes are co-seated with AP classes.

Approaches To Learning (ATL): a systematic development of learning skills: communication, collaboration, organization, self-management, reflection, research, informational literacy, media literacy, creative and critical thinking.

Assessment Criteria: Four equally weighted criteria with eight possible achievement levels. Each level has unique descriptors for teachers to use to evaluate student work.

Areas of Knowledge (AOKs): are in effect disciplines in which knowledge may be based. Certain knowledge may overlap certain AOKs or not fit well with any of them, however most knowledge and specific disciplines taken into consideration during the course do fit.

Business and Management (BM): a group 3 course

Cambridge University Press (CUP): a very good publisher of textbooks

Candidate: this is the term used by IB to refer to students who are in the IB diploma program; they are candidates for the IB diploma until their exam results are finalized, usually after graduation.

Candidate number: every IB candidate is assigned a candidate number. You will need to know this for your exams and also to access your results.

Creativity, Activity and Service (CAS): a requirement for the IB Diploma. Student learning and experiences outside of the classroom. 18-month commitment to exploring areas in creativity, activity and service.

Certificate: A document issued by the IBO once a student has taken an IB exam for an IB course.

Coordinator: the title of the person who oversees the day-to-day operations of the IB program, arranges schedules and examinations, advises students and communicates the IB philosophy to students, faculty and parents.

Collaboration: The act of working with others to achieve shared goals. Teachers will specify when collaboration is appropriate

Collusion: The act of allowing someone to copy your work and take credit for it

Course Student: A junior or senior student who is not working toward the IB Diploma but is taking an IB course and therefore is taking an IB exam.

Diploma: Students taking six IB subjects are pursuing the IB Diploma, sometimes called the "full Diploma."

Descriptors: These are course-specific expectations or criteria for performance evaluation used by the teacher. They exist in every subject to aid in the grading of IAs.

Diploma Candidate: A senior student who is completing the requirements for the IB Diploma.

DP: International Baccalaureate Diploma Programme, a two-year comprehensive programme, designed for ages 16 – 19 or grades 11 and 12.

Error Carried Forward (ECF): seen often in mark schemes

Environmental Systems and Societies (ESS): a group 3 and 4 interdisciplinary course

Extended Essay (EE):- a requirement for the IB Diploma. The EE is a 4,000-word research paper.

External Assessments (EA): These assessments are graded by trained IB examiners. External assessments include the written IB exams taken by the student at the end of a DP course, normally in their second year of the Diploma Programme. In some courses, including film, the external assessment is a textual analysis. In visual arts, studio work is assessed.

Group Subjects: IB students are required to take classes in six subject areas: 3 higher level and 3 standard level:

Group 1: Studies in Language and Literature.

Group 2: Language Acquisition

Group 3: Individuals and Societies

Group 4: Sciences

Group 5: Mathematics

Group 6: The Arts

GDC: Graphic Display Calculator

Haese and Harris (H&H): publisher of math books

Higher Level (HL): HL courses are taught over two years and include a rigorous study of the course material. These courses allow students to explore areas of interest within the subject in greater depth when compared to SL.

Internal Assessments (IA): IB required assessments provided by the teacher.. Depending on the subject the IA could be oral exams, projects, essays, experiments, case studies, etc. that are scored by the teacher. IB externally moderates to ensure quality. A randomly selected sample of these assessments are sent to IB to ensure that the IB teacher is scoring according to the IB rubric.

IB: International Baccalaureate (also IBO, International Baccalaureate Organization)

International Baccalaureate Information System (IBIS): an online IBO platform for organizing and submitting student, staff, and school information to IBO

IB Diploma: A document issued by the International Baccalaureate Organization once a student has earned the minimum number of points after completing the requirements for the IB Diploma.

Individual Oral (IO): in Language and Literature courses (group 1), worth 30% at SL; 20% at HL. It's one of the three coursework requirements you'll need to complete for IB English (both for SL and HL).

Information and Technology in a Global Society (ITGS): a Group 3 subject

Investigative Workbook (IWB): for Visual Art, the sketchbook / journal

TOK Prescribed Titles (PT): These titles are published around six months before the submission deadline, so on September 1st. You choose one to write your TOK essay about, using two AOKs (areas of knowledge).

TOK Prompts: needed for the TOK exhibition. You choose one out of the 35 to guide your exhibition.

Learner Profile: The IB learner profile is a list of traits that the IB wishes to nurture in its students. These traits are centered around international-mindedness, inquiry, and reflection.

Learning Outcome (LO): a task's aim

ManageBac (MB): is the leading planning, assessment and reporting platform for the IB continuum.

Marks: IBO's language for grades given to internal and external assessments as well as exams.

Markscheme (MS): The answer key for the past paper – very important documents

Mathematical Exploration: The IA for group 5 mathematics course

Moderation: This is the process of evaluation for internal assessments (IA's) used by an appointed IB assessor. Moderation ensures that the IB's reliable global standards are maintained at all IB World Schools.

MLA (Modern Languages Association): a common way of formatting bibliographies and citations. This is the citation style that we recommend for all students.

MYP (International Baccalaureate Middle Years Programme) designed for ages 11 to 16 or students in the 6th through 10th grade.

Orals: Students in English A1 (Group 1) and Language Acquisition (Group 2) must complete oral presentations. These presentations are sent to IB examiners for assessment. (Students in Film and Visual Arts complete a similar process.)

Oxford University Press (OUP): very good publisher

Paper: IBO's language for an exam in a subject area. An IB exam is never just one exam, but rather a series of "papers," often administered over the course of two days.

Predicted Grade (PG): IB teachers submit to IB their prediction of the grade the student will earn in their IB subject. Students normally do not see these grades, nor do they figure in their ultimate IB grade in the subject. They are used for initial acceptance to university in countries other than the United States.

Prescribed Literature in Translation (PLT): an official list of literature published by the IB for use in Group 1.

Presentation Planning Document (PPD): document you need to fill out for your TOK presentation.

Pre-IB: courses designed as preparation for the DP (varies school to school)

Questionbank (QB): searchable online databases containing hundreds of examination questions, markschemes, and subject reports that align with the current International Baccalaureate syllabi for various subjects.

Research Question (RQ): For the Extended Essay, you choose a research question as a topic

Scores: Scores for IB exams range from 1 – 7, 1 being the lowest score and 7 being the highest. Scores are determined by points assessed by the various components for the exam, then broken down into defined ranges for each score of 1 – 7.

Both TOK and the Extended Essay are awarded letter grades and depending on one's grades in these two requirements, students may earn up to 3 bonus points, applied to their total Diploma score.

Subject Guide (SG): a very important document that you should consult at the start of your program – contains all the things you will need to learn.

Standard Level (SL): A course study of study consisting of less depth and breadth when compared to a higher-level course. It should consist of 150 hours. Many courses are one year in length, but some do occur over two years. (Students may take up to two SL tests after one year of study. This is dependent on course availability and student level of study in a subject area.) A diploma student must take 3 HL courses and 3 SL courses over the junior and senior years.

Texas Instruments (TI): calculator manufacturer; many IB students use a TI-84 or TI-nspire.

Teacher Support Material (TSM): a very important document that teachers use for administration of their course. Contains helpful information on IA procedures and sample work.

Theory of Knowledge (TOK): A requirement for the IB diploma. TOK is the IB Diploma Programme capstone course, which asks students to reflect on the nature of knowledge. This course integrates all six subjects with the goal of teaching students that all knowledge is related.

Contributors

Do YOU want to contribute to the next edition of this book? We are always looking for talented and insightful IB students (current and alumni) to improve and add onto this book.

Zouev Publishing

For more information on publishing your IB material, please visit www.zouevpublishing.com, where you can find our other range of IB books also. We are also interested in obtaining individual chapters on subjects not yet addressed in this book, so don't hesitate to get in touch if you feel like you have something to contribute – we would be happy to collaborate.

For any questions or comments, please email us at zouev.publishing@gmail.com

IBTutorOnline

For potential tutoring opportunities, please visit www.ibtutoronline.com

IBSurvivors

For further resources and guides, visit

www.ibsurivors.com

Author Contact

To reach Alexander personally, please email

alexander.zouev@gmail.com

To reach Inessa personally, please email

ineskulbuni@gmail.com

To reach Annique personally, please email

anniquequarles@gmail.com

www.ingramcontent.com/pod-product-compliance
Lightning Source LLC
Chambersburg PA
CBHW011549070526
44585CB00023B/2516